Living with severe aphasia

The experience of communication impairment after stroke

Susie Parr

Edited by Sally Byng, Carole Pound and Alan Hewitt

The Joseph Rowntree Foundation has supported this project as part of its programme of research and innovative development projects, which it hopes will be of value to policy makers and practitioners. The facts presented and the views expressed in this report, however, are those of the author and not necessarily those of the Foundation.

Living with severe aphasia

The experience of communication impairment after stroke

Susie Parr

Edited by Sally Byng, Carole Pound and Alan Hewitt

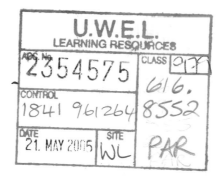

Pavilion

RESEARCH *INTO* PRACTICE

JR 1904 2004
JOSEPH ROWNTREE FOUNDATION

RESEARCH *INTO* PRACTICE

Living with severe aphasia

Susie Parr

Edited by Sally Byng, Carole Pound and Alan Hewitt

Published for the Joseph Rowntree Foundation by:

Pavilion Publishing (Brighton) Ltd
The Ironworks
Cheapside
Brighton, East Sussex BN1 4GD

Telephone: 01273 623222

Fax: 01273 625526

Email: info@pavpub.com
Web: www.pavpub.com

The Joseph Rowntree Foundation
The Homestead
40 Water End
York YO3 6LP

Telephone: 01222 303150

Fax: 01222 560668

First published 2004

ISBN 1 84196 126 4

Editor: Catherine Jackson

Cover illustration: © Caroline Firenza

Design and typesetting: Jigsaw Design

Printing: Paterson Printing (Tunbridge Wells)

Contents

Acknowledgements

This project was dependent on the input of many people. First, we would like to thank Alex O'Neil for his unwavering support and good sense. The members of the project advisory panel contributed many hours of work and numerous insights. We would like to thank Lynne Andrews, Colin Barnes, Judith Duchan, Cressida Laywood, Jayne Lindsay, Geof Mercer, Tony Moor and Carol Watson, and for their invaluable guidance. We wish to acknowledge the speech and language therapists and those working in the voluntary sector for their efforts in helping us locate possible participants with aphasia, as well as all those who took the time to respond to the survey. Numerous service providers from the statutory and voluntary sectors appear in this study. Their contribution was central to the project and we wish to thank them. Caroline Firenza provided the illustrations for the project, and we would like to thank her. Finally, and most important, to the people with aphasia and their families who took part in the project: thank you.

Chapter One
About the project

Aphasia is a language and communication difficulty that commonly follows stroke. Many people with aphasia have difficulty understanding written or spoken language and expressing themselves in speech or writing. Severity of aphasia can vary enormously. Some people experience such profound loss of language that their ability to communicate in any form at all is severely restricted. It is estimated that there are at least 40,000 people with aphasia living in the UK.

How the project began

In 1994 we embarked on an innovative research project (also funded by the Joseph Rowntree Foundation) that aimed to find out about aphasia from the perspective of those affected. Fifty people with aphasia, of different ages and backgrounds, were recruited to talk about their experiences in in-depth interviews. The project culminated in the publication of a book, Talking about Aphasia (Parr *et al*, 1997). Most respondents were able to express themselves in some way, using a combination of speech, writing and gesture and with support from the interviewer. Wary of exclusion, we also asked a small number of people with very severe communication difficulties to take part. It quickly became apparent that their interviews were rather sparse in comparison with the in-depth accounts given by other respondents. In effect, people with severe aphasia were excluded from participating fully in the research because the methodology was not suitable.

The realisation that people with severe communication difficulties were excluded from Talking about Aphasia prepared the ground for the project that is the subject of this report. We became increasingly aware that many people with severe aphasia sit silently in day centres, nursing homes, rehabilitation units and their own homes, their day-to-day experiences, thoughts, feelings and concerns unexplored and unknown. They seemed 'unheard', 'forgotten', 'invisible', 'difficult to reach'. We started to plan a study that would document the day-to-day experiences of this group of people and explore (as far as possible) their perspectives on life with aphasia, tracking the processes of social exclusion as they occurred. We joined forces with Colin Barnes and Geof Mercer from the University of Leeds. Their work in the field of disability studies suggested they would bring challenging theoretical perspectives as well as practical experience to this project. We are grateful to the Joseph Rowntree Foundation for funding this study and supporting us throughout the long and sometimes difficult process of trying to find out what life is like without language and communication.

We considered different qualitative methodologies that might allow us some way to explore the experience and perspectives of people with severe aphasia. Ethnography seemed to have the most potential. Ethnography is a long-established method that has its provenance in the field of social science. Once the tool of western anthropologists exploring remote and exotic communities, in recent decades the method has been used to analyse the nature of groups and practices closer to home and to document the experience of vulnerable and marginalised people. Lately ethnography has become a more overtly politicised tool, used to effect social change (Hammersley & Atkinson, 1995). Ethnography is both a process and a product. It is an eclectic and flexible methodology, combining observation, interaction, artefactual analysis and interview. It allows experience, behaviour and meaning to be explored in naturally occurring contexts.

Ethnography has been identified as a useful means of studying healthcare. Savage (2000) contends: 'As a detailed way of witnessing human events in the context in which they occur, ethnography can help healthcare professionals to solve problems beyond the reach of many research approaches, particularly in the understanding of patients' and clinicians' worlds.' Our desire to explore the experience of people with severe aphasia was underpinned by our intention to identify the processes of social exclusion and inclusion, with the long-term aim of being able to influence and challenge these processes.

Ethnographic methodology raises numerous complex ethical issues, in particular around consent, transparency and representation. However the emphasis on observation and artefactual analysis as well as interview and interaction made ethnography seem the most appropriate method for exploring the day-to-day life of people with severe aphasia, for whom verbal communication is extremely problematic.

The architecture of the project

An overview of the project might be useful at this point. **Table 1** below shows the sequence of events.

The table makes the project seem neater than it actually was. It was originally intended to run for two years but in the end it stretched to three. Throughout, perhaps inevitably, a series of difficulties made the whole process more time-consuming than we had envisaged at the start. These concerned the labour-intensive nature of ethnography, our unfamiliarity with the method, the mass

TABLE 1: Stages of the project		
Month	**Aspect of the project**	**Project infrastructure**
1–6	Set up advisory group Develop and conduct survey Negotiate ethical approval for ethnographic study Start recruiting for ethnographic study	Advisory panel meetings
7–18	Conduct ethnographic study	Advisory panel meetings
18–24	Conduct interviews with family members/carers Carer diaries Begin ethnographic data analysis Analyse survey data	Aphasia working party meetings analysing data
24–30	Continue ethnographic data analysis Analyse interview data Commence write-up Develop accessible report	Aphasia working party meetings analysing data Advisory panel meeting
30–36	Feedback to aphasia working party Feedback to participants Refine write-up Write accessible report	

of detailed data, the ethical dilemmas mentioned above, issues around involving, informing and engaging people with communication difficulties in the process of research, and struggles with reflexivity and our role in the project.

It seems important not to ignore these dilemmas, and yet they should not obscure what was actually achieved. With this in mind, the rest of this chapter will be taken up with descriptions of the methodologies used in the main components of the project: the survey, the ethnographic study, the interviews with carers and the artefactual analysis. In the next chapter the processes, meetings and consultations that formed the infrastructure for the project will be described and discussed, along with the issues around inclusion, ethics and reflexivity. **Chapter 3** gives a summary of the findings from the various components of the project, and in **Chapter 4** we draw these together and discuss them in terms of social exclusion.

The survey of people providing services for those with severe aphasia

Given the narrow focus of the study – the detailed documentation of the day-to-day lives of 20 people with severe language difficulties – we decided to try to complement the microcosmic ethnography by gaining a more general idea of 'what happens' to people with severe aphasia across the UK. With the help of members of our advisory group, we developed a survey for speech and language therapists, voluntary organisations and organisations of disabled people that asked them about the nature and scope of their contact with people who have severe aphasia. We also developed a separate, more accessible survey that was sent out to self-help groups of people with aphasia. In total, 506 questionnaires were sent out.

Content of survey

The survey was designed to elicit both quantitative and qualitative information about respondents' contact with people who have severe aphasia and the service they provide. It was also aimed to elicit respondents' views of the natures of the obstacles facing people with severe aphasia, and how these might be surmounted. The survey contained questions about the following issues:

- the type and organisation of the service provided by the respondents and the population served
- the respondents' definition of severe aphasia
- the number of people with severe aphasia using the particular service
- how and when people are put in touch with a service
- what type of service is offered and for how long
- the domestic situation of people with severe aphasia known to the respondents
- the respondents' perceptions of obstacles facing people with aphasia
- strengths and weaknesses of services
- difficulties that might be experienced by people with severe aphasia in using services, and how these might be remedied
- main ways in which services might be improved
- main ways in which the quality of life of people with severe aphasia might be improved.

The respondents in the aphasia self-help groups were likely to have aphasia themselves, so the lengthy questionnaire was adapted, shortened and made more accessible for this group, with input from two members of our advisory group. This means that the data from the self-help groups, while addressing broadly the same issues, are dealt with separately in this report as appropriate.

The findings from survey are described in detail in **Chapter Three**. They provide a useful backdrop to the detail of individual experience documented in the ethnographic component of the study and give a national perspective on the issues explored in localised settings and in minute detail.

The ethnographic study

Ethnographic data capture naturally occurring phenomena in rich detail, collected from multiple sources and analysed at different levels. These data are drawn from different methods: chiefly participant observation, complemented with interview, interaction and artefactual analysis. The detailed data gathered as a result of these endeavours provide a micro-cosmic picture of everyday experience. Minute description of the mundane, taken-for-granted world can 'illuminate the habitus of socially constructed values as these are embodied and played out' (Edgar & Russell, 1998).

The detailed nature of ethnography makes it extremely labour-intensive. Such in-depth study is only practicable with small numbers of people (20 in this case). We decided to locate the search in one urban area in the UK. This was to ensure the planned programme of observational visits was viable and manageable.

Gaining access to participants

Following the negotiation of ethical approval in three adjacent healthcare trusts, the first task was to find 20 people who would be willing to take part in the study. Given the nature of their communication impairment, initial contact was made through established networks: speech and language therapists, voluntary and self-help groups, and organisations dedicated to supporting people

after stroke. Following a series of phone calls, letters and visits explaining the project and the sampling criteria, these contacts approached possible participants on our behalf, sounding out their feelings about possible involvement. If the signs were positive, an appointment was made for us to visit, explain the project and ask for their consent to take part, using specially developed materials (pictures and keywords) to back up the information. A copy of this information is included at **Appendix One**. Relatives and carers were also given information sheets and asked to sign consent forms.

As in any small-scale qualitative study, the aim was to access a cross-section of people with severe aphasia who would represent a range of different factors and experiences. A sampling matrix was set up. Quotas were set for sampling criteria, including age, gender, type of aphasia, home circumstances, level of physical impairment and ethnic origin. The sampling process involved trying to find people who would fit those criteria. Unwilling to put people through testing, we did not ask our therapist contacts to recommend people who only scored below a certain level on tests of aphasia. Instead we asked people to consider those who, in their opinion, had major difficulties with communication as a result of aphasia.

This strategy seemed effective in prompting speech and language therapists and some of the voluntary sector contacts to think about possible participants. However day centre and residential and care home staff found it difficult to identify people with aphasia-related communication difficulties. None of these contacts referred to medical or care notes: they simply scanned their own thoughts and memories. Critically, none seemed to know the term 'aphasia'. People with severe communication difficulties would be recommended, but their difficulties were often associated with motor impairments or dementia, not aphasia. It was difficult to describe exactly the sort of person we wanted to contact without using off-putting jargon. It was also hard to give tentative and conditional explanations to some of the possible participants without raising their expectations or making them feel anxious or rejected.

Eventually 20 people were found who were identified by our contacts as having severe and intractable communication difficulties following stroke and who seemed interested in the project. I ascertained as far as possible on my first visit that they did indeed have aphasia, and also that no other major influences were affecting their communication (such as deafness, dementia or severe motor speech impairment). This was usually done without any recourse to medical or other notes, simply by talking to the person concerned and to family members and carers, hearing about how the trouble had started and analysing their communication informally. This process was more difficult in the institutional and some voluntary settings I visited, as often nobody knew much about the people concerned. **Table 2** overleaf shows some of the characteristics of the 20 people with severe aphasia who took part in this study.

All the participants finally selected were judged to have aphasia following stroke. In trying to classify the participants, the type of aphasia is divided into two broad categories: those with relatively fluent speech (but poor comprehension), and non-fluent speakers for whom every utterance was a struggle. However within these two categories each person was different, experiencing different difficulties and making use of different resources. Styles of communication varied. Each had adapted to aphasia in different ways, finding their own means of communicating and using various devices and means of support. Some used drawing, gesture or mime, intonation and bits of writing to supplement their speech. Some

were able to use word lists to some effect. Three were trying out a portable communication aid, with varying degrees of success. Some had no resources on which to draw. The nature of communication also depended on the interlocutors: what they did and said. People with aphasia met with many different responses.

A question about the study that is bound to arise concerns the type and severity of the aphasia experienced by the people who took part. Like Allen (2001), we were unwilling to put our participants through any form of testing, as this would run counter to the inclusive ethos of the project. Judgement of 'severity' was therefore based on subjective estimates of the degree of difficulty in communication. In an initial advisory group meeting Cressida Laywood (who has aphasia herself) asked how it is decided whether someone's aphasia is severe or not. The answer, that this was generally judged through formal testing of language skills, met with some incredulity. Cressida pointed out that people with what might seem to be relatively minor language difficulties often experience these as seriously disabling, and vice versa. This point is central to the project and will be re-visited in the concluding chapter of this report.

It proved particularly problematic to find younger people with severe aphasia, and also to trace people from ethnic minority groups. In the event, two people in the study are of Afro-Caribbean origin. The difficulty finding younger people may arise from the fact that the incidence of stroke increases with age. Two people in their 30s were finally found, both of whom had had strokes a matter of months before the start of the project.

Sadly, two participants died early on in the project. Others were found to take their place. More recently, Harry, Albert and Fred have also died.

The process of giving information and gaining consent was complex and time-

TABLE 2: Information about the participants

Name and age	Years since stroke	Type of aphasia	Physical impairment	Domestic situation	Source of contact
Roger, 50	3	Non-fluent	None	Home with family	Voluntary organisation
Pete, 53	2	Non-fluent	Marked	Home with wife	SLT
Ruth, 33	1	Fluent	None	Home with family	Person with aphasia
Donald, 71	2.5	Non-fluent	Marked	Home with wife	SLT
Gill, 55	12	Non-fluent	Marked	Home with husband	Voluntary organisation
Brenda, 72	3	Non-fluent	Marked	Nursing home	SLT
Ivy, 72	5	Non-fluent	Marked	Home with husband	SLT
Frank, 79	6	Non-fluent	Severe	Home with wife	SLT
Albert, 91	1	Non-fluent	Severe	Nursing home	SLT
David, 60	2	Non-fluent	Severe	Home with wife	Voluntary organisation
Jean, 74	1.5	Non-fluent	Severe	Home with husband	SLT
Charles, 59	4	Non-fluent	Marked	Home with wife	Day centre
Harry, 81	1	Fluent	None	Home alone	Voluntary organisation
Terry, 54	12	Fluent	None	Home with wife	Voluntary organisation
Anthea, 80	2	Fluent	Marked	Nursing home	SLT
Mary, 53	6	Non-fluent	Marked	Home alone	SLT
Miss Silver, 77	15	Non-fluent	Marked	Home with family	Day centre
Fred, 78	12	Non-fluent	Severe	Nursing home	GP
Christine, 74	1.5	Non-fluent	Severe	Home with husband	SLT
Tom, 38	9 mths	Fluent	Marked	Home with partner	SLT

SLT = speech and language therapist

consuming. Every effort was made to design project information that would be accessible to someone who struggled to read and understand. A number of drawings were commissioned to illustrate and explain aspects of the study (**Appendix One**). I spent a lot of time going through this material with each person, trying to ensure they understood what the project was about and what would happen.

Participant observation: organising visits

Each of the 20 people with severe aphasia was visited three times during the course of the study. I planned to spend time with each person in different settings and situations. This was in line with the time-sampling strategy described by Hammersley and Atkinson (1995). In some cases it was impossible to vary the setting because the person was at home or in the same room all

TABLE 3: The settings and situations observed in the ethnographic study	
Person	**Settings and situations**
Roger	1. Going to the local post office alone to buy cards and stamps 2. Playing in a bowls match 3. At home with wife and family
Pete	1. At home with paid carer, then going to the pub with family 2. In day centre 3. At home with wife
Ruth	1. In day centre 2. Shopping at Tesco's 3. At home with family
Donald	1. At home with wife 2. Occupation therapy session in hospital 3. Visit from friends, doing singing practice
Gill	1. At home and at a local stroke club 2. Local shopping and visit to Lidl's supermarket 3. Swimming
Brenda	1. Having lunch in dining room of nursing home 2. In room, watching TV 3. Meant to be bingo, but cancelled. Watching tv in room
Ivy	1. At home with husband 2. Taking part in a stroke group at a day centre 3. Having hair done by a home care worker
Frank	1. At home with family 2. In respite care setting 3. At home with family
Albert	1. Having lunch in the nursing home 2. Sitting in alcove in nursing home 3. In own bedroom at nursing home, unwell
David	1. In day centre doing cookery 2. At home with wife and visitor 3. At local stroke club
Jean	1. At home with husband 2. At home, daughter and granddaughter visit 3. At home with husband
Charles	1. At day centre, having lunch and taking part in a quiz 2. Physiotherapy session in hospital 3. At home with wife
Harry	1. At home alone 2. At stroke club 3. Shopping at Sainsbury's with son-in-law
Terry	1. At day centre, working on computer 2. In respite centre 3. At home alone
Anthea	1. In room at nursing home 2. In room at nursing home 3. In room at nursing home

continued...

TABLE 3: The settings and situations observed in the ethnographic study *continued...*	
Mary	1. At home alone 2. At Different Strokes meeting 3. At home alone
Miss Silver	1. In day centre, doing crafts 2. In day centre, eating lunch 3. In day centre, taking part in Christmas service
Fred	1. Having lunch in dining room of nursing home 2. In room watching tv 3. In room at nursing home, unwell
Christine	1. At home with husband 2. At home with husband 3. At home with husband
Tom	1. At home with partner 2. Outpatient occupational therapy 3. Going to the pub with partner

the time. Some people were physically frail; others had chosen to stay put. However I would try to choose a time to visit when something was going on in the setting: for example a relative might be visiting, or some activity might be going on. Each visit lasted between one and three hours. **Table 3** above shows the different settings and situations that were observed.

Participant observation is a deceptively simple process. It involves the observer entering a situation and watching and recording whatever is going on. At the same time, as the word 'participant' implies, the observer is not always detached or removed from what is going on but becomes a part of the activity, as and when appropriate. In this study, sometimes it was possible for me to sit and make notes unobtrusively and without interacting much with the various people in the setting. This was particularly the case when something else was going on: for example, therapy or computer sessions or recreational activities such as quizzes. Often, however, my engagement was inevitable and I became involved with activities: for example, helping to carry in shopping from the car or joining a swimming session (when it was very difficult to make notes!). Most often I engaged in conversations and interactions,

particularly when visiting a person who was on their own. Documentation of these conversations became a part of the data.

Participant observation: writing field notes

Spradley (1980) has identified some categories to guide observational note-making that are helpful in ensuring attention to a broad representation of events:

- space: the physical place or places
- actor: the people involved
- activity: a set of related acts people do
- object: the physical things that are present
- act: single actions people do
- event: a set of related events that are carried out
- time: the sequencing that takes place over time
- goal: the things people are trying to accomplish
- feeling: the emotions felt and expressed.

As explained in the project information, on every visit I scribbled notes whenever I could, trying to attend to the above categories: particularly what was said, which I noted down verbatim. Although initially uncertain about how people would react to this, it soon became a matter of course. No one ever objected or seemed put out by my constant writing: indeed, to my surprise, they hardly seemed to notice.

We had debated making audio or video recordings during observational visits: an issue that is discussed in depth by Hammersley and Atkinson (1995). While acknowledging the strength and detail such equipment might bring to observational data, these authors also point out a number of disadvantages: the inevitably selective focus; the loss of vital information (perhaps not recording something happening in a corner, out of earshot or audio view); necessary attention to the recording or filming process interfering with observation and participation; possible negative impact on participants, and the huge resource needed to analyse such data adequately.

Although we had obtained consent to use these methods, once the visits started it quickly became apparent that they would contribute little to the process of gathering the detailed, subtle and comprehensive information that already seemed to be available. Using such equipment would probably have resulted in restricted access to some activities and settings. While nursing homes, day centres and rehabilitation units seemed happy to allow me to visit with my notebook, making a video or a tape-recording was another matter. Last, the act of visiting vulnerable people at home already seemed potentially intrusive; every visit had to be carefully and delicately negotiated so that peoples' feelings about it were checked out. I was concerned that using video or audio equipment in such sensitive situations would be upsetting for the participants and counter-productive for the project. So, in the end, I stayed with pen and paper. This clearly raises a number of issues about selection, interpretation and representation. These will be discussed in **Chapter Two**.

Immediately following each visit, several hours were spent expanding the hastily scribbled notes, writing a detailed account of the events that had just been observed. At this stage a very preliminary form of analysis was begun: points in the text that seemed of possible theoretical interest were highlighted and considered under the heading 'Interpretative notes'. No attempt was made to classify these issues at this point; they were simply noted and queried. At the same time, if any methodological issue seemed important – for example, a sense that a particular question should be explored further in the study – this too was pointed out.

The final level of expanded notes started to incorporate explicit reflexivity into the research process, as my personal notes on the text started to take shape. Sometimes I was aware during observations and writing sessions that an issue was affecting me personally. These issues included worries about my own health and my family, and reflections on my personal and professional experiences. Rather than try to obliterate these personal perspectives, ethnographers are now encouraged to be explicit about their involvement. Reflexivity adds to the authenticity of any ethnographic work, underlining the premise that there is no external reality, only multiple representations and meanings (Davies, 1999).

Sixty visits over the course of the project resulted in 60 sets of expanded and detailed notes, annotated with interpretative, methodological and personal comments. An example of one page of the notes is given in **Appendix Two**, and some excerpts from them appear in this report.

Analysing the ethnographic data

Analysis of ethnographic data begins with the organisation of field-notes into categories. Data are scrutinised and sorted into themes to provide the infrastructure for searching and retrieval. This can be done in numerous ways, using different forms of indexing and coding. Computer software can be useful but, as Hammersley and Atkinson (1995) observe, manual sorting is still perfectly appropriate and often a more flexible way to begin analysis. Generally, the types of categories developed undergo some changes as the research proceeds and the process takes on the characteristic 'funnel' structure: starting wide and progressively narrowing. These changes mark the gradual focusing of the enquiry, generally towards some theoretical implications, although some ethnographic studies remain heavily descriptive.

In this study, the process of analysis was complicated. The entire set of notes was carefully read and discussed by some members of the research team. People with aphasia who were members of the advisory group also met and discussed some notes. This process will be described in more detail in the next chapter. These initial discussions led to some strong reactions: for example, feelings of shock, upset and sadness were expressed, not just by people with aphasia but by everyone involved. At this point it felt difficult to get beyond these immediate and powerful reactions and move towards more conceptual analysis. The mass, detail and intense narrative nature of the data felt overwhelming.

Data were sorted in terms of some categories that would allow a more abstracted and organised view. Conceptual categories suggested by Layder (1993) provided a basis and for the analytical process.

- *Self, identity, narrative*
  - What conceptions of self and identity are bound up with certain kinds of activity?
  - What meanings and perceptions are bound up with these activities?
  - How are these meanings expressed? Verbally? Non-verbally?

- *Situated activity and interaction*
  - Who is doing what to whom? Forms of manipulation, persuasion and control?
  - Are there patterns of behaviour that emerge over time?
  - What social functions do these patterns serve?
  - What forms of communication are used? Verbal? Non-verbal? Both?
  - Irony? Humour? Particular terminologies?
  - How does setting influence the action?

- *Setting*
  - What is the nature of the setting?
  - What is the nature of relationships within these settings? Pecuniary (that is based on a financial arrangement)? Emotional? Service-based?
  - Is there evidence of hierarchy and control? Do some groups and individuals control other groups and individuals?
  - What resources underpin these relations of power and control?
  - To what extent do conflict and tension characterise these settings?
  - How are tensions resolved?
  - To what extent do issues of gender, class, and race impinge on the settings?

- *Context*
  - What is the distribution of power and resources most relevant to the activity?
  - What values, ideas and ideologies encourage or discourage certain forms of behaviour?

With these concepts in mind, analytical charts were developed and the data from the notes sorted into different headings and sub-headings. The charts allowed data to be organised under the following broad headings: actors and activities; settings; interactions; identity and narrative, and the exercise of power and ideology in all these domains. An example of such an analytical chart is shown in **Appendix Three**. The charts formed the basis for a set of chapters that explored these domains in detail. At this point, all names and some identifying details were changed, to ensure anonymity.

Finally, returning to the original research question, markers of social exclusion and inclusion were identified and illustrated from the notes. These fell into four broad interacting categories: infrastructure and resources; the behaviour of other people; settings and environments, and personal identity and narrative.

This last analysis provided the basis for returning the findings to members of the aphasia working group and to participants. At this point the focus fell on issues of social exclusion and inclusion and attempts were made to represent these concepts in an accessible format. The discussions that occurred in these consultations constituted another form of data in themselves and led to a further simplification and revision of themes, with suggestions for implementing change. The final chapter of this report captures these essential concepts.

Interviews with family members and carers

There was some debate at the start of the project about whether or not the views of the relatives and carers of people with severe aphasia should be a part of this study. It was argued that their voice might be privileged over that of people who struggle to talk. These issues were troublesome, yet it seemed important to try and describe the lives of people with severe aphasia in context, not isolated from those around them. We wanted to attend to the subjective experience of severe aphasia, as far as this could be explored, but also to try to understand how other people behave and feel towards those for whom communication is so difficult. As

the observations continued it became clear that people with severe aphasia are exposed to many different social contacts, in a range of contexts. People react very differently to communication trouble, explaining it, working out what it means and finding different ways of dealing with it. Sometimes people seemed to enable and include the person with aphasia, but often the opposite was true. Increasingly, it seemed a good idea to try to explore some different peoples' perceptions of severe aphasia through interview.

Eighteen people (three of whom were paid carers and the rest family members) therefore took part in in-depth interviews exploring their perspectives on aphasia. Interviews were audio-recorded and transcribed, then analysed using the Framework method (Ritchie and Spencer, 1994). Interview data were scrutinised alongside the observational data and fed into the analytical framework and into the final analysis.

Artefactual analysis: documents and diaries

A range of artefacts in the form of written documents was collected where possible, or transcribed verbatim, whenever they were encountered in the day-to-day context of people with severe aphasia. These included: literature produced by institutions such as nursing homes, respite and day centres, and by different services; letters from different agencies; notices; written instructions, and mission statements. Documents were also solicited, in the form of diaries. Family members were also invited to keep a diary for a week and to record in them what had happened, who had come into contact with the person with aphasia, what had been said, and any struggles or problems around communication that had emerged. Although 20 diaries were sent out, only seven were returned. Some family members made it clear that they did not have time to complete the diaries.

Hammersley and Atkinson (1995) suggest that such artefacts provide a rich source of topics for analysis. They suggest some good questions to ask of such documents: how are they written? how are they read? who writes them? who reads them? what is recorded? what is omitted? what does the writer take for granted about the reader? what does the reader need to know to make sense of them? These questions stimulated an analytical perspective on the documents and artefacts that accorded well with the overall data analysis and fed into the conclusions about social exclusion and inclusion.

Conclusion

Despite its seemingly narrow focus on the everyday lives of a small number of people with aphasia, this study was neither simple nor straightforward. Careful attention was paid to developing the different components of the study, the varied methodologies, the intricacies of data production and analysis and the complexities of representation and validation. The data took a narrative form that at times felt impenetrable to those who read or heard it. In addition, a major dilemma emerged. The project was about social exclusion. Would the process of research, like so much disability-related research, consolidate the exclusion of the people it was about? How could the research process be inclusive? These questions will be addressed in the next chapter.

Chapter Two

Inclusive research with people who have aphasia: potential and pitfalls

'After much critical reflection on my own work during the 1980s, provoked by my involvement in the disability movement, I came to the inescapable and painful conclusion that the person who had benefited most from my research on disabled peoples' lives was undoubtedly me.' (Mike Oliver, in Barnes & Mercer, 1997)

Much has been written in recent years about changing the social and material relations of disability research. Mike Oliver's admission above, and his critique of researchers who use disability as a means of promoting their own careers, prompted a discourse on the nature, purpose and ethics of disability-related research: who drives such research, and who benefits from it? Initiatives in research that are driven by, inclusive of and useful to disabled people are now, if not commonplace, at least in evidence. These mirror similar initiatives promoting the involvement of users in healthcare research.

Zarb's (1997) honest account of a research project in which disabled researchers were employed revealed some of the major practical and structural barriers to participation in research for disabled people. But what other barriers exist? In particular, what issues arise when the tools that are essential to the research process are compromised by impairment? Language is the medium of research. Research is generated, implemented, analysed and reported using language. What are the opportunities and obstacles to involvement in research for people with communication and cognitive impairments, who face many language-related barriers? These issues are now starting to be addressed more consistently. Recent initiatives focusing on the empowerment of people with dementia and people with learning difficulties, for example, have shown how it is possible to develop designs and methods that are more inclusive of those for whom language is a struggle (for example Allen, 2001; Townsley et al, 2002).

As far as we were aware at the start of this project, no research had been undertaken that was inclusive of people with aphasia, other than our own attempts in previous projects. We were clear from the start that this project was not initiated or driven by people with aphasia but by us, the non-disabled researchers. We wanted to ensure that the research was conducted in accordance with the following principles:

- that the process should be as inclusive as possible of the people it was about

- that the outcomes of the project should indicate some means of bringing about beneficial change

- that people with aphasia should have a role in influencing the way the project developed.

Some of these aspirations were easier to meet than others. This chapter discusses some of these issues.

Including the 20 participants

It is often difficult for people with aphasia to understand written and spoken information, to ask questions and to express wishes and concerns. The participants in this project all had major difficulties with written and spoken communication. This raised an enormous challenge. How is it possible to inform and include in research people for whom written and spoken communication is so difficult?

Strategies for making the research process more inclusive developed as the project proceeded. These comprised:

- the creation of accessible project information and consent materials
- the development of accessible feedback materials and final report
- attention to how these materials were used with participants
- accessible communication with participants throughout the course of the project
- different methods of engaging participants in feedback and validation.

Creating accessible materials

Careful attention was paid to the development of accessible information, consent and feedback materials (**Appendix One**). In these materials participants were addressed directly, as 'you'. The purpose and form of the project was spelled out in clear terms. Language was simplified and stripped of jargon. Sentences were shortened. Key words were emphasised. Text was enlarged. Layout was streamlined and spaced out. Key points were illustrated using specially commissioned drawings. Expectation of written responses was minimised and responses made as straightforward as possible (for example, ticking a box by an illustrated option). These materials were discussed with the advisory group.

Developing feedback materials for participants was a difficult process. Immense amounts of complex data were synthesised and condensed into a limited set of key points. Feedback materials were designed to present these, using continua to show different aspects and levels of exclusion and inclusion. These materials were complemented by illustrations showing scenarios and vignettes from the data. Participants were invited to use these materials to reflect on their own experience and to locate their own sense of exclusion or inclusion.

Updates were sent out to participants at intervals throughout the project. Again attempts were made to ensure these were as accessible as possible, using the above methods. The final, communicatively accessible report is being designed to convey the findings in a straightforward way: that is, divided into clear sections, using simple language and layout and supplemented with illustrations. The report will use diagrams, illustrations and stories to convey some of the aspects of social exclusion and inclusion experienced by people with severe aphasia.

Use of accessible materials

Great care was taken in using the above materials with the 20 participants. Each person was guided through the project information at their own pace, any questions or concerns were facilitated and their comprehension and consent were carefully checked. When it came to getting feedback on the project from the participants, the initial plan was to work with the people with aphasia at their own pace in their own homes. However it proved very difficult to achieve a genuine consultation with the person with aphasia. Naturally enough, family members were also interested and wished to be informed and involved and to comment on the issues raised. It proved very difficult to manage the feedback sessions so as to ensure the views of the person with aphasia were heard. On reflection, it seemed the participants with aphasia might be enabled to express their views more easily if facilitated and supported feedback was organised for them as a group, and a separate feedback process organised for family members and carers.

As a result, two feedback meetings were organised, to which participants were invited. Transport was arranged and travel expenses were met. The feedback meetings were planned to allow participants with aphasia to discuss the findings in small groups, apart from family members and carers, at their own pace and with skilled facilitation and support. Materials were refined on the basis of these meetings and participants' comments and reactions were fed into the final report.

Including the project participants: some pitfalls

Although undertaken with the best intentions, the above strategies for inclusion could not resolve the dilemma that lies at the heart of this project. Despite every effort to convey the nature of the project in the consent process, it was not clear that participants fully understood the detail of what would be involved and exactly how their lives would be scrutinised and reported. This was partly because, of course, we did not know ourselves at that point precisely how the study would turn out. The ethnographic data, captured as they were in expanded field notes and narrative texts, were not accessible in those forms. In addition, the accessible report represents a simplification and distillation of the complex findings of the project; it strips the project down to broad themes. Many subtleties, and the more tentative interpretations, are lost.

Another ethical dilemma arose around the issue of consent. The project ostensibly focused on people with aphasia and their families (who gave their consent for the project to go ahead), but as fieldwork progressed it rapidly became apparent that the activities and interactions of the vast number of people who featured in the participants' everyday lives were also important. Paid carers, rehabilitation workers, group members, volunteer helpers, tea ladies, assistants, nurses: the circle of interactants was unexpectedly extensive. Their words and actions came under just as much scrutiny as the words and actions of the people with aphasia. Incidental encounters and conversations were noted, and analysis of these has been fed into the conclusions of this study. The focus widened from people with aphasia to those who populated their social world. Unexpectedly, these people became participants in the project too.

Including members of the advisory panel

One of the requirements of the Joseph Rowntree Foundation is that grant-holders should convene advisory panels to guide and monitor their progress throughout projects. For this study, we planned that such an advisory panel should meet every few months over the course of the project to hear about progress and discuss developments. Given the focus and ethos of the project, we wanted to involve people with aphasia in this role, and particularly to include some people with severe communication difficulties. We therefore invited five people with aphasia to join the research team on this panel. Although all the people with aphasia had difficulties using spoken and written language, the communication of three panel members was severely compromised. None could speak, other than the occasional word. Writing was also problematic: mostly they wrote single words or fragments of words. Each person struggled to understand complex, rapidly spoken language and found most forms of written text incomprehensible. Each person expressed their thoughts and feelings in different ways, using a combination of speech, writing, body language, intonation and facial expression.

At the first advisory meeting, in which academic researchers met with the people with severe aphasia, we were hopeful that an inclusive advisory process would be achievable. To start with, we adapted two main aspects of the advisory process: the information and support materials and the structure and organisation of meetings. As the project developed and we began to ask more of advisory panel members, we had to be flexible and try out different ideas.

Information and support materials

These were distributed to every member of the panel, including those who did not have aphasia. Agendas, minutes and briefing notes were adapted and made as accessible as possible, with large text, stripped down language, emphasised key points, spacious layout and specially commissioned illustrations (for example, showing the entire group meeting or split-off groups, calendars and clocks, and lunch).

Changing the structure and organisation of meetings

To make the advisory group meetings as accessible as possible to people with severe aphasia, we adapted the structure and organisation of meetings. Rather than cramming everything into a two-hour period, we stretched the meetings so that hour-long periods of work and discussion were interspersed with breaks. This aimed to minimise fatigue and overload. Right at the start the group set ground-rules for all participants. These included giving people time, not rushing, not speaking over others,

talking slowly, using straightforward language, avoiding academic and technical jargon, and checking that points had been understood before moving on. We issued each person with aphasia a red card, the idea being that this could be held up to suspend a discussion that had become too fast or overwhelming. Rather than working all together, we worked in small groups over short periods, ensuring that people with severe communication difficulties were supported in each group. In addition, we tried to incorporate a system of summarising and re-capping what had been discussed at the end of each session.

Two skilled facilitators joined the meetings, acting as communication supporters for those with severe aphasia. This required them to sit next to the person with aphasia, capturing key points of the discussion in writing and checking that the person understood. They also signalled and interpreted any contribution, reading what the person with aphasia was writing and formulating and checking out whatever was being conveyed.

As the project developed, an increasing amount of information had to be fed back to the advisory group and discussion points became more complex. A dilemma arose around how to share the ethnographic data with people with aphasia on the panel, as none of them could read through such vast amounts of detailed description. We decided together to adapt the way in which we met to try to make possible some access to the data.

Adapting meetings: the aphasia working party

The people with aphasia met separately from the other advisory group members to discuss the data. A series of three meetings of the aphasia working party was organised over a two-week period. Each meeting ran from late morning to early afternoon, with a break for lunch. Some of the field notes were audio-recorded and tapes were sent out to each person, together with the written text for those who wished to have this. Forms were developed for working party members to note down their responses to the tapes. The tapes were then discussed, with facilitation, at the meetings. The data from only three sets of visits were discussed in this way over the three meetings. Two members of the working party claimed payment from the Foundation for this work and successfully negotiated with the Benefits Agency to keep their fee. Other working party members did not wish to have payment for their contribution. In at least one case this was because they feared losing benefits.

Including the advisory panel members: some pitfalls

Numerous difficulties arose during the advisory process. These took a number of different forms. It was clear at the first meeting of the entire panel that it was going to be hard to avoid tokenism in this setting. It proved hard for some members of the panel to adapt their communication, to interact naturally, to slow down and to resist using academic language and theoretical jargon. As debates got going the pace invariably quickened, but the red cards were not used. This may have been because they were discriminatory, as they were only held by members of the panel with aphasia, or perhaps because signalling in this way was awkward and unfamiliar – we did not find out. The meetings proved tiring for everyone, and difficult to chair and mediate.

For people with aphasia, there seemed to be considerable confusion about the role of the advisory panel. Some people wanted to become more involved: for example, in carrying out some aspects of the research, coming on visits or helping with feedback. In addition, it was difficult for people to detach their advisory role from their personal experience. The nature and purpose of the advisory role had been stated in broad terms at the beginning of the project, but was re-visited and re-negotiated as the project progressed whenever misunderstandings seemed to arise. However meetings were too infrequent and far apart for people to keep hold of discussions about the role of the advisory group. The ethnographic nature of the project led to uncertainty about 'what the project is about', with a desire for more clarity about the intended outcomes and outputs from the research at an early stage.

There was some, occasionally heated, debate about the ethics of involvement and the control of the research, which stemmed from dissatisfaction with the necessarily limited role of the advisory panel. The fact that there was only one project worker, and that the worker did not have aphasia, was a continuing source of tension. The reality that the research process is necessarily language and communication based poses an ongoing dilemma about both the employment of people with aphasia as project workers and their close engagement in the research process, which this project did not address. We discuss this issue further below. This tension was addressed directly in smaller meetings between group members with particular concerns and members of the project team.

Another difficulty arose with the pace of the project. Fieldwork was labour-intensive and frustratingly slow, and there was little contact with advisory group members between meetings, with the result that advisory group members with aphasia often lost the thread of what was happening. Things went much better when a series of meetings was held close together, bringing a sense of impetus, pace and connection. In addition, group members with aphasia struggled to get to grips with the nature of ethnographic research. The data were overwhelmingly detailed, and it was difficult for everyone involved to see how any conclusions and points for action might be gleaned from this mass of loosely narrative information. One question was asked repeatedly: 'What is this research about?'

This sense of disorientation eased somewhat when the findings were presented in a fairly compact and manageable way at the feedback sessions. The expressed wish of working party members was that the research should 'do something' and 'be useful'. The slow process of gathering, sorting and distilling the data and the tentative nature of some of the findings proved a frustration in this respect.

There were issues around access to all the data that mirrored the problems of involving the 20 participants. In their raw form the data were inaccessible. In their accessible form they were stripped back. Members of the smaller aphasia working party only accessed a small proportion of the entire data set. They had a strong and accurate sense that they did not know about all the other data – data to which non-aphasic members of the panel had full access. In addition, the accessible minutes, although attempting to convey points raised in a meeting in a straightforward and economic way, often failed to capture the intricacies of a discussion. Members of the advisory panel experienced for themselves numerous small, sometimes subtle moments of exclusion.

Alan Hewitt, a member of the aphasia working party and the advisory group, who helped to edit this report, commented on the uncomfortable feelings raised by the fact that he had access to the data and the report because he could read. Other members of the aphasia working party didn't have this access, because reading was more problematic. Alan described his position as 'an ongoing problem. An insider and an outsider'.

How might the research process be made more inclusive of people with aphasia? The lessons learned from this study are invaluable and perhaps applicable to research with other disabled people, not just those who have aphasia. With hindsight, the most important learning point was that inclusive principles cannot be just an add-on but should influence the development, design, timing and resourcing of the research process right from the start. The Foundation was generous and flexible in supporting the changing plans for facilitating involvement, and this did go some way to opening up the research to people with aphasia. With hindsight we can see that we would have benefited from allocating further build-up time to the development of the research questions and proposal, so that collaboration could be fostered and shared 'ownership' of the project established at the beginning. In addition, a prolonged 'wind-down' time would mean that findings could be explored in a more extended and meaningful way, both with participants and with advisors. In this way, adding 'wings' to the design of a project such as this, on either side of the main body of the research process, would perhaps foster the confidence of people with aphasia, enabling their genuine contribution to the process and discussion. There are considerable resource and management implications here.

One of the problems identified by the aphasia working party was that fieldwork was conducted by a non-aphasic researcher alone. Could the involvement of a person with aphasia have made the study more 'real' and authentic? Ethnography is language based and demands a combination of intense, sustained attention, stamina and flexibility on the part of the ethnographer. These features make it difficult, but not impossible, to envisage how a person with aphasia might be included in conducting the research in a non-tokenistic way. Such a role would again demand considerable planning and resources: training, flexible transport, longer build-up times to visits, briefing and de-briefing sessions and time for the ethnographer to analyse and add in the person's interpretations to the data set. Inevitably the process of research would become slower, and a degree of flexibility and spontaneity (for example, arranging a visit at short notice to fit in with an event) would be lost.

Concerns about the process of gaining informed consent might be allayed if it were to become more iterative. This would mean returning to people at each stage of the project to ensure their understanding and consent, rather than assuming consent for the whole project on the basis of one meeting right at the start.

Once fieldwork was under way, advisory meetings became relatively infrequent. On reflection, it might have been useful for everyone, including the researcher, to have regular feedback meetings during this time, in which progress was reported and discussed. More regular updates could perhaps have taken different forms, perhaps backed by a communicatively accessible project newsletter sent out to all interested parties. More opportunities to access and react to the data would perhaps have strengthened panel members' sense of orientation within the project (and this, perhaps, could have been supported by repeated reference to a visual timetable). In addition, training for non-aphasic advisory group members, focusing on how to enhance communication access, would have been helpful.

We have learned from other initiatives in which people with aphasia have contributed their views and experience to a planning process or taken part in a research project that it is critically important to be clear and absolutely explicit about what the project is about, what is going to happen, where and when, and what is being asked, and to create a highly structured programme of

consultation and feedback meetings. This structure often requires preparatory work to support discussion, such as a preliminary 'brain-storm' to give people examples from which to work. Making ideas or information concrete in this way seems to enable people with aphasia to grasp more tangibly what a discussion is about, or more specifically what they are being asked to give an opinion on or make suggestions about. Great care has to be exercised by any facilitator so that options are not closed off and important issues omitted. Such processes could perhaps be monitored by someone from outside the project. Such endeavours are resource-hungry in terms of planning and preparation time, materials and skill.

Strategies like these would not automatically make a project inclusive but could perhaps provide the framework for starting to change the social relations of research production. The role of an advisory panel seems to be at stake here. The sorts of strategies outlined above might enhance involvement in and ownership of a project and might enable active, creative and authentic contributions, rather than comments from a distance. Critical issues around respect, confidence, power, trust, inclusion and access were opened up in the way this project was run. Interestingly, they reflect some of the issues emerging in the findings.

Including myself: some thoughts on reflexivity

The process of conducting an ethnographic study demands reflexivity on the part of the researcher. Reflexivity means that the researcher is not as an objective presence but is an explicitly acknowledged source of questions, values, insecurities and experience, all of which feed into the research process, thereby enriching and elaborating the data set (Davies, 1999). That any research process is value-driven, not neutral, should be openly acknowledged from the start (Hammersley & Atkinson, 1995). This impinges on the social relations of disability-related research (Barnes *et al*, 2002.) It also raises a number of interesting and important debates around the nature of science, objectivity and bias and 'levels of evidence.'

This project was intrinsically value-laden and value-driven. It originated in experiences of and concerns about the social exclusion of people with severe aphasia, and from a desire to produce research that would be useful to people who are its subject. While this might raise questions about its objectivity, the study was conducted systematically, transparently and with rigour: features that underpin its scientific basis.

Throughout this project I have aimed to be reflexive: that is, to make clear my values, concerns, assumptions, fears and questions, and to make transparent the fact that I am doing so.

To me, one of the strengths of the ethnographic process is that it allows theme and theory to be explored and demonstrated in the mundane. It can show how processes such as social exclusion (and social inclusion) actually occur in day-to-day settings, conversations and encounters: the 'taken for granted' world. Far from being a matter of brutal oppression, social exclusion is often played out in subtle cultural forms: how one person addresses another, how a notice is worded, how a room is organised. Ethnographic study can capture such details and subtleties in the taken-for-granted world and allow their significance to be explored and articulated.

Chapter Three

Findings from the ethnographic study, interviews with carers and the survey of service providers

This chapter outlines the main findings from three components of the study: the ethnographic field-notes, the interviews with carers and the survey.

The ethnographic study

The ethnographic study was the main focus of the project and absorbed the major part of research effort and time. Three extracts from the observational notes (below) give a taste of the nature of ethnographic writing. The field notes constitute a comprehensive narrative concerning everyday life with severe aphasia. Each of the 60 visits to people with aphasia was documented: protagonists, activities, interactions, artefacts and environments were all observed and described.

'Do you want soup, Brenda?' asks the nurse. 'NO,' Brenda says very firmly and puts her hand over her mat. She makes her face express disgust. Her purse and a glasses case are lying by her mat. The nurse doesn't give her any soup and gives some to the woman on her left, who lifts it from the mat and puts it into the centre of the table. It is getting very hot. There is a smell of urine. Brenda looks flushed. She looks at me, makes the same disgusted face again and then smiles.

The whiteboard by the door has today's menu written on it in felt tip pen and it says this is chicken soup. I see a nurse at another table where three women are sitting; she is pouring the soup from the plastic cups into ceramic bowls and giving it to them. This doesn't happen for anyone else. The soup doesn't look or smell very appetising. It smells like packet soup and the appearance is not helped by the plastic cups, which are much the same colour as the contents.

Artefact

The leaflet on the home says the following:

'Comfort and service
Excellent catering and a wide menu choice provided by a qualified chef using in-house facilities and fresh produce.'

Then she dries Gill's feet and helps her with her tights and her calliper. A conversation is going on between the three helpers. Gill is silent. They discuss whether there is any one to take over the swimming group. All three of the helpers go over to the mirror and comb their hair while Gill puts her towels and costume in her bag. The woman who is due to retire says: 'I had my hair cut and I really don't like it…' and the others talk about how difficult it is to find a hairdresser you like. Gill walks over to the mirror. She rummages in her bag and pulls out a sweet that she puts into her mouth. She listens to the haircut conversation then turns to me and points to herself and then to her hair. 'You were a hairdresser?' I say and she nods. I say to the woman: 'Gill is saying she was a hairdresser' and the woman nods and says she knows and that Gill knows all about hair. Gill lifts up some strands of the woman's hair, her head on one side, then turns the woman round to face the mirror and lifts up some strands at the back, then smoothes down some strands behind her ears. She looks at the woman's reflection in the mirror, her head on one side. 'You could have done it for me couldn't you?' says the woman and Gill nods. Then she gets a comb out of her bag and starts to comb her own hair, looking at herself in the mirror. The others start to leave. The physio goes: 'Goodbye goodbye.' She doesn't say goodbye to Gill, who is still combing her hair, only to the other two women and to me.

During the quiz, the nurse suddenly turns to Pete. 'Can you write it down?' she says. 'Do you want to? You can join in.' 'No no no,' he says. 'Yes, but no.' 'It'll take too long?' 'No yes, but...' 'It's too much trouble?' 'No yes, but um…' 'It's not too much trouble for me. I'll fetch a pen and paper.' She goes out. Pete looks at me, still the same smile. She comes back in with one small piece of paper and a pencil. 'There you are.' 'No no no,' he says, smiling and shaking his head. 'What about yes yes yes?' she says. Everyone starts to laugh and there is a chorus of 'No no no' and 'Yes yes yes'. Pete takes the pencil and sits with it poised over the paper on the table, leaning forward, his gaze on the nurse. He is smiling.

There follows a summary of the key issues arising from the ethnographic notes. The subtle and descriptive nature of the data is lost when they are cooked down into summary form. A detailed account of the ethnographic component of the study will be published elsewhere.

The protagonists

While aphasia was the focus of this study, it is important to point out that other factors have a profound impact on peoples' experience. A number of people in the study experienced physical problems as a result of stroke. These included paralysis, incontinence, difficulty swallowing, seizures and headaches. For some, medication had a negative effect, making them very fatigued or nauseous. Those who attended day centres or therapy sessions or who lived in nursing homes were steeped in institutional life. Given these factors, it seems impossible to disentangle the effects of aphasia from those of living with restricted mobility or living in an institution, or feeling depressed or unwell. Aphasia does not occur in a vacuum and cannot be studied in isolation from other factors.

It can be seen from the table overleaf that people with severe aphasia often operate within large and complex social networks, both informal and formal. It was surprising how many people entered the sphere of the study, aside from the 20 main protagonists. Family members, friends, neighbours, therapists, nurses and other healthcare workers, volunteer supporters, home aides, day centre and nursing home staff, other people with stroke, aphasia and other impairments, and ancillary staff such as tea ladies, drivers and assistants all entered the social domain of the person with aphasia. Paradoxically, although isolation was one of the issues that seemed problematic for everyone with aphasia in the study, this often occurred within the context of extensive social contacts.

Each of the 20 participants had a rich and diverse personal history, of work, education, family life, achievements and aspirations. Family members often supplied information and built up a detailed picture of the person and their lives together. Evidence of the past was also found in photographs on walls and

TABLE 1: People featuring in the study

Person with aphasia	Family member or paid carer	Others who appear
Roger, aged 50	Wendy (wife)	Son William, daughter Sally and grandchildren Alfie and baby Rose; bowling club members; post office worker; woman walking dog
Pete, aged 53	Ann (wife)	Day centre staff and clients, particularly the manager (Cath) and the nurse; son John; friends in pub; Bill, the home care nurse
Ruth, aged 33	Wid (husband)	Daughter Kerry; day centre staff and clients; shop assistants
Donald Fell, aged 71	Mrs Fell (wife)	Two occupational therapists; their patients; the friend who collects him from the hospital; the singing friends; the man who came to mend the wheelchair
Gill, aged 55	Fred (husband)	Shop assistants; the shoplifters and their possible accomplice in the car park; volunteers; other people attending the swimming club and stroke club; stroke club organiser; man in pub
Brenda O'Farrell, aged 72	Nurse	Other residents; nurses; the managers of the home; care attendants
Ivy Clifford, aged 72	Mr Clifford (husband)	Day centre clients and staff; the volunteer; Barbara, the Crossroads worker
Frank Stock, aged 79	Mrs Stock (wife)	Daughter Janet; toddler grandson Adam; respite ward staff
Albert Cotton, aged 91	Elderly persons' home: no one	Other clients and their relatives, including the man who went to school with Albert; staff; people at funeral; the minister
David Brown, aged 60	Mrs Brown (wife)	Cookery teacher; Cathy, the person in charge of supporting people with communication difficulties at the day centre; volunteers, organisers and people attending the stroke club; the visiting friend
Jean Turner, aged 74	Mr Turner (husband)	Daughter Carol and granddaughter Emma
Charles Green, aged 59	Mrs Green (wife)	Day centre staff and clients; the physiotherapist; her assistant; her patients
Harry Painter, aged 81	Catherine and Douglas (daughter and son-in-law)	Shop assistants; others attending the stroke club, particularly Freda; Julia, the organiser; volunteers
Terry Dixon, aged 54	Sheila (wife)	Matthew who runs the computer room; day centre staff and clients; respite centre staff and clients, particularly Steven; the driver; other passengers on the bus; the tea ladies
Anthea d'Olivera, aged 80	Elderly persons' home: nurse	Residential home care staff
Mary Livingstone, aged 53	No one	Jim, who heads the Different Strokes meeting; the trainer; other members of Different Strokes

continued…

TABLE 1: People featuring in the study *continued*		
Miss Silver, aged 77	Gloria (daughter)	Janice, who heads the Caribbean day centre; other clients; the craft worker; care staff; the Reverend Jones and other church personnel; the congregation at the service; teenage granddaughters who interrupt the interview with Gloria; Gloria's brother
Fred, aged 78	Social services elderly persons' home: care attendant	Other residents at the meal; the care attendant who serves them; the unseen resident who objected to Fred; the administrator
Christine Jacobson, aged 74	Mr Jacobson (husband)	No one
Tom Sweeney, aged 38	Jacqui (partner)	The occupational therapy staff – John the assistant and Pippa the boss; other clients in the woodworking room; friends in pub

in albums, and in personal documents such as letters and certificates. From these it was often possible to learn something about family, friends and personal history, particularly when family members were present to interpret and add information. With communication support and perseverance, it was possible to learn a lot about the person with aphasia. But those living in nursing homes did not have this support, and family and friends were not around. Nursing staff and key workers often had no idea about their past lives. Unable to speak or communicate, people with aphasia became stripped of their history and context.

Settings and environments

Sitting sometimes for hours with people who cannot communicate, my attention was drawn to the environments and settings in which they passed their time. I documented the appearance, sounds, smells and feel of places, noting how and where people with aphasia were seated, and how the space was used. The following points emerged.

Institutional environments

Sometimes people with severe aphasia are physically set apart and sequestered from others, particularly in institutional environments. Although this happens to other people too, those with aphasia may not be able to call for attention or initiate a conversation. The three people observed in nursing homes spent most of the time alone. In some institutional settings people who can't communicate may have little control over their environment: warmth, light, tv, radio, the way a room is organised and decorated. People with aphasia can't always ask for a light or radiator to switched on, a channel to be changed, a radio to be fixed or a picture or chair to be moved. Noise is a major issue in institutional environments. It is particularly intrusive and distracting for people with aphasia, yet seems to be an unnoticed part of institutional culture. Noises are often ignored by staff: phones ringing, someone repeatedly calling for attention. Staff often add to noise levels by calling or shouting across rooms, crashing equipment and turning on or turning up background music.

Sometimes institutional environments displayed a confused identity. For example, some settings seemed to be part hotel, part hospital, as clinical equipment and institutional smells co-existed with swagged curtains, standard lamps and comfy chairs. While attempts to make institutional environments more comfortable and homely are to be welcomed, confused identities were often apparent in the way day-to-day life contradicted publicity material and mission statements. For example, Albert sat alone for hours each day in an alcove in his nursing home; no one had any contact with him other than to offer him tea and to take him to meals, to the toilet and to bed. Yet the institution's mission statement describes a caring and inclusive ethos, in which residents are encouraged to participate in the home community.

How notices and posters are phrased can be very revealing of underlying institutional attitudes towards clients and residents. The person with severe aphasia may be represented and addressed as a customer, a patient, a disobedient pupil, an inmate.

> *I look at the notices on the wall next to the hatch. They are pinned everywhere, notices about notices: 'Please take note of the notice on the right: Please do not question staff re other patients' food. It is not your business about others' dietary needs.' 'If at any time the food is not to your liking, please bring your own.' 'Bridge View wheelchairs are not to be taken off the Unit.' 'If the payphone rings, please answer it. It is not the responsibility of the staff.' 'Important notice: Please note this is not a communal facility. As such it is expected that all clients are in bed by midnight to cause minimum disruption to clients.'*

While some institutional environments (for example, Brenda's room in the nursing home) were well cared-for, clean and organised, with good quality fittings and furniture, many were shabby and seemed poorly maintained. Frank's room in the respite centre was hot and smelly, there was no remote control for the elderly television, the radio was broken, and the un-watered pot plants on the window sill were dying. At home Frank enjoyed radio and tv, but in respite care these forms of entertainment were not available or accessible. He spent each day of his fortnight's respite sitting in a room on his own, with nothing to do and unable to ask the staff for help. When I asked a member of staff what Frank did all day, she replied: 'Not much.'

Domestic environments

Some people living at home experienced housing problems (dereliction and poor maintenance; vandalism; high rates of burglary and drug abuse). There was evidence of difficulty and delay acquiring aids and adaptations at home. Often equipment provided didn't fit or failed to meet needs in the home setting. Sometimes there was a mismatch between therapies and what was actually going on at home and the difficulties that arose. For example, because he could not use the stairs and had no stair lift, Charles was forced to live in the tiny ground-floor living room, all the space taken up with his bed, armchair, commode and the sofa. His physiotherapist had not seen his home situation for herself and chastised him for not practising walking, which he had no space to do. He often misunderstood her and could not tell her about the problems he was experiencing. People adapt, problem solve, figure out their own ways of doing things to get around mobility and communication problems. Often their solutions are idiosyncratic and unconventional, bearing little relation to what therapists recommend.

Day-to-day life: routines and rituals

I documented the day-to-day activities of people with aphasia, at home and in institutional and care settings. I also described the various activities that went on in therapy, day and respite care and voluntary groups.

Some people with severe aphasia sleep a lot, taking naps during the day. People in institutions, and some people at home, go to bed very early. For some, the routines of physical care take up a large proportion of the day. The person with aphasia and family member often engage in these rituals in silence – the carer attending to nail-clipping, hair-washing, shaving, preparing and delivering meals. Mealtimes provide an important structure for the day, as does the television. Watched in isolation, tv can be a companion, provide conversation and allow the person to engage with the outside world. Watched with another, tv can be a shared activity and stimulate conversation and comment. It's important to be able to control the tv and the radio, and this was often a problem in institutional settings.

Aside from the routines of care, eating and watching tv and going to various day care and therapy sessions, people with aphasia have little to do during the day. Many carers commented that visitors seldom came after the first few weeks and were not sure how to engage with the person with aphasia. The few social visits witnessed were often structured and formulaic: for example, when three friends made their weekly visit to do some singing practice with Donald in the hope of helping him produce some speech sounds. Sometimes helpers can't think of anything that will break through the tedium: each morning Pete's nurse was at a loss as to how to relieve Pete's evident boredom. Conversation seemed impossible. One or two carers enabled people with aphasia to engage in absorbing, enjoyable and purposeful activity: sports, listening to music or talking

books, or sharing in housework, cooking and shopping. However such opportunities were limited. Usually things like shopping were done for people with aphasia, and without them being there.

When attending therapy, day-care or voluntary groups, people spent a lot of time, sometimes many hours, waiting for transport to pick them up or take them home. In contrast with life at home, therapy and day centre sessions were filled with activity, usually under the direction of the person in charge. The purpose of therapeutic activities was not always made clear. Therapists didn't seem to attend to explanation and negotiation as much as they did to keeping activity going. Sometimes therapists used jargon and didn't explain clearly what they were doing and why. Sometimes it seemed that what went on in therapy did not correspond with the life issues faced by the person. If people don't fit in with therapy agenda, they are considered unmotivated and likely to be discharged. People with aphasia often have to take part in activities they don't enjoy, that they find boring, or to which they cannot contribute. They have no opportunity to negotiate what happens.

Interactions

Communication, or lack of it, was a central focus of this study. I documented the ways in which people interacted with those with severe communication difficulties. Communication breakdown is tiring and uncomfortable for everyone. Frustration often arises when communication breaks down. People with aphasia get exhausted. Sometimes they prefer to give up rather than struggle on with making a point. We know that there are ways in which people with severe communication difficulties can be supported to express themselves and engage in conversation (Kagan, 1998), by using and encouraging gesture, drawing and writing key words, and by systematically checking understanding and meaning. This is not easy. I found that it works best when you can sit down at a table and talk in a relaxed way to the person, with paper and pencil within reach. It is much more difficult to support conversation when walking along a street with someone, or in a brief, spontaneous exchange, or when under pressure.

One or two family members were able to support the communication of the person with aphasia (for example, changing their questions, 'homing in' on the topic and encouraging the person to use writing and drawing). But in healthcare and institutional settings there was virtually no evidence of efforts to support communication. Sometimes this had potentially dangerous consequences. For example, when Frank went into respite care his wife left instructions about means of communication, together with a warning that he should not be given liquids to drink as he was in danger of choking. Nursing staff did not read these notes and did not know how to communicate with Frank, who was offered tea. He was able to indicate that he did not want it, but it was only some time later that staff understood the situation.

How people speak and interact with people who have aphasia varies. Formulaic and ritualistic interactions are very common, and may lift pressure off the need to communicate. People often used jokes and repetitive banter ('You behave yourself! None of that carrying on!') as a way of easing communication difficulties. This can be a very limiting form of communication, and sometimes demeans rather than includes the person with aphasia. People often develop different theories and strategies for trying to resolve communication breakdown. Sometimes people tried to teach the person with aphasia to speak, suggesting they needed to try harder and were being 'bad'. Fred's key worker made him try to repeat

the name of every item of food and clothing before she gave it to him, believing this was good for him. Some people minimised their communication: for example, one care assistant in Albert's nursing home gave him single word commands, like a dog ('Sit.' 'Back'). Some, particularly those running therapy sessions and quizzes, used authoritarian language and issued strings of instructions and evaluations. But many just sidelined or over-ruled the person with aphasia, who, after all, cannot complain.

Pete is still waiting. He sits in his wheel-chair patiently, outside the empty office. 'You waiting for Cath, Pete?' 'Yes.' 'She'll be here soon,' says the woman in pink.

Then up comes the woman who was outside drinking tea. It's Cath, I realise. 'Hallo Pete, you alright?' she says loudly. She is standing in front of him, looking down at him. 'Yes. No, Yes…but er…oh… Yes.' 'You going to tell me about next week?' 'Yes, yes, but em…' 'You're not coming in next week?' (All this in a loud voice while she stands next to his chair in the busy corridor.) 'No, no, um um um and er…'

'Shall I give …what's her name…what is it… Ann… Shall I give her a ring?' 'Yes… er…no, um, um, um, but…yes…' 'Hang on a minute…I'll give her a ring…' she says. 'Yes…yes.' he says and she turns away. The conversation is finished. Cath doesn't go into her office but starts to look at the clothes that are for sale in the lobby. Pete sits for a minute, looks over to me with a smile and a quizzical expression. He shrugs slightly.

Sometimes protagonists talked to people with aphasia in such a way as to make them seem different and mark them out as being a 'special case': someone in need of care and protection. This was conveyed by loud, slow, sing-song speech, exaggerated intonation and particular body language: for example, stooping over the person and laying an arm around their shoulders. Sometimes ways of addressing people with aphasia suggested that they were not competent adults or people with thoughts and feelings. They often seemed to become invisible, referred to as 'he' or 'she' in their presence. A particular example occurred when Brenda, sitting in a queue of people waiting for the lift back up to her room, wanted to go the toilet. When this was pointed out to a nurse, the nurse said: 'We take them all up at once. They all go up at once. We know it's not that desperate. She went just before lunch.'

There were one or two examples in which family members and paid workers instinctively interacted with people who had aphasia in a natural, inclusive way, engaging them in conversations, stories and jokes. Some relatives were extremely sensitive to the attitudes of others, and to their behaviour and interactions with the person with aphasia. One or two highly skilled communicators had energy and humour and were able to conduct conversations for two in such a way as to draw on the person's contributions and incorporate them seamlessly into the dialogue.

Healthcare and other staff have a great deal of day-to-day contact with people who have aphasia, yet they may not have the time, skill, knowledge, resources or training to support and include them. This is particularly a problem in institutions such as day centres and nursing homes where the workload is heavy, cultures of care are rarely questioned, staff are poorly paid, staff turnover is rapid and the opportunities for training and support are limited. Confronted with communication problems, people independently devise strategies and produce communication aids that they think will be helpful but which are often unsuitable and unusable.

Narratives

Narratives are accounts of episodes and incidents, but also interpretations and versions of events. This study, a narrative in its own right, explored the narratives of different people with severe aphasia and those around them through observation and interview.

Different aspects of narrative emerged: for example, the importance of story telling as a means of dealing with unpleasant events such as trauma and illness. Gill and her husband Fred were verbally abused by a young man in a supermarket car park because they accidentally touched his car. Fred and I were able to talk over this episode and tell people about it. But Gill could not do this, although she engaged very closely with our narration. Because it usually depends on language, narrative can be hard for people with aphasia. Often their version of events is not heard. With skill and sensitivity, people with aphasia can be supported in the act of narration. Telling stories is important and may enable communion, respect and social well-being. It is possible to involve a person with aphasia in the telling and sharing and hearing of stories, as Barbara, who came to do Ivy's hair, demonstrated. Even though Ivy could not say a word, she was engaged in a long, satisfying chat about Barbara's family life.

Together, Roger and Wendy narrated the story of her life-threatening illness, with Roger miming the dramatic events that unfolded as she got sicker and sicker, and then the phases of her recovery. Wendy quickly verbalised what Roger was expressing through his facial expression and actions. He complemented and acted out her words.

But individual narratives or interpretations of events may conflict. People with aphasia, partners, families and institutions may tell very different stories and interpret things differently. Tensions were often evident in the images and metaphors used by relatives. For example, some carers talked about the person with aphasia not as a competent adult, worthy of respect, but as a burden ('I have to drag him out to the shops'), a child, a mechanism that had broken, even as a dog. Others stressed the essential humanity and personhood of the one with aphasia, despite the loss of communication.

Institutions create powerful narratives concerning illness, recovery, disability and rehabilitation and the nature and purpose of the services they offer. Sometimes these narratives are at odds with the views of the people served. The occupational therapy assistant explained that the purpose of woodwork activities, such as painting bookends or making key hooks, was to make people feel they had achieved something worthwhile and enhance their self-esteem. Yet for Tom, desperate to return to work as an electrician, they were boring and pointless. Often people who struggle to communicate cannot convey their history, experience, views and aspirations. In many cases institutional workers seemed to know very little about the people with aphasia for whom they cared and the issues they were facing, and had no idea how to find out.

The points summarised above indicate the disabling impacts of profound aphasia but also the potential for people with aphasia to be engaged and included. These issues will be examined in more detail in **Chapter Four**, with reference to more examples from the ethnographic observations.

Findings from the interviews with family members and paid carers

Eighteen people agreed to take part in in-depth interviews in which they talked about their experience of caring for people with severe aphasia. Three of the interviewees were institutional carers: two nurses and one care worker, all working in nursing homes and each with special responsibility for a person with severe aphasia. Family members were interviewed at home; I travelled to the institutions to interview paid carers. Unsurprisingly, interviews with close family members were often lengthy, lasting up to two hours. In contrast, interviews with institutional carers were short, partly because they were often under pressure to return to work and partly because there was often relatively little to say as they did not have previous knowledge of the person with aphasia. Interviews were audio-recorded and transcribed, then analysed using the Framework method (Ritchie & Spencer, 1994). Interview data were scrutinised alongside the observational data and fed into the analytical framework and into the final analysis.

The interviews with relatives and paid carers offered valuable information and insight into the experience of severe aphasia, and brought home how aphasia affects not just those who have it but also those around them. The following account summarises the perspectives and narratives of family members and paid carers. It covers three broad areas: accounts of the stroke, treatment and recovery; perceptions of aphasia and the ways in which people react to it, and the impact of aphasia and stroke on the life of the person affected and those around them.

Accounts of the stroke, treatment and recovery

Family members gave affectionate and detailed accounts of the person before aphasia entered their lives: their work and leisure interests; their relationships with children and grandchildren; their roles in family and community life; their plans and aspirations; their quirks, foibles and talents. These rich accounts are in stark contrast to the sparse descriptions given by institutional carers:

> 'I don't know a thing about his past.
> I've only been here about two years
> and he was in before I came.'

As indicated above, many institutional carers only knew the person with aphasia. But family members gave dramatic and detailed accounts of the event that brought many changes into their lives. They spoke with intensity about the immediate aftermath of stroke and the days, weeks and months that followed. For many, the physical and communication effects were quickly apparent, yet it was impossible to discuss what had happened with the person at the centre of the crisis. Carers described the sense of turmoil and being too overwhelmed by events to take anything in. Some experienced a sense of isolation, powerlessness and abandonment, even at this early stage:

> *'Nobody came and asked me how I was coping. Nobody did it, not a soul, and I just felt as if I was drowning really.'*

For some, full realisation of the effects of stroke came gradually. Fred took a while to realise why Gill was unable to talk: he thought she couldn't speak because of the tracheotomy tube in her throat. Lack of explanation meant that David's wife took months to realise the reason for his difficulties with communication:

> *'No one told me that he couldn't speak, that he'd lost his speech. I thought he couldn't speak because he didn't know who I was. I didn't find out for months after he came home. No one thought to say to me he might never speak.'*

On top of all the uncertainties and worries, many carers were trying to negotiate with employers and trying to sort out their immediate financial situation. There was real hardship, with little help to hand: *'I didn't know where the next penny was coming from.'*

Even within this small sample, recruited as they were from the same geographical area, type and intensity of treatment following stroke varied enormously, both in the acute setting and in the community. Some had long-term, regular support; others were seen only fleetingly. One common experience was the sense that speech and language therapy began to tail off when little progress was made. Therapy 'lapsed off', 'fizzled out', 'dwindled away', 'kind of died off.'

The time of return from hospital to home was when the relatives were confronted with the aftermath of stroke. As well as dealing with physical aspects of care, many were grappling with their changed financial situation and negotiating the benefits maze, and there were few for which this was not a traumatic and stressful experience:

> *'They say no, you've got to keep filling it in until you get it right, which is wrong. Because you waste months and months of misery. And frustration.'*

> *'Oh dear, that was a nightmare.'*

Gradually hopes of recovery of communication skills started to fade. People adapted to this in different ways, some living in a state of suspended animation as they watched their relatives:

> *'I'm waiting for Ruth to switch herself back on again.'*

Others started to think that this situation was how it was going to be:

> *'This is life. This is it. 'Til I die. I don't know, 'til she dies. I don't know. This is life.'*

Wendy described how hard it was to reconcile an honest appraisal of the outlook with hopefulness:

> *'They say to me: "It will come back." Well if it does that would be wonderful. But you cannot spend your life, you just can't. You come to a point where you just have to accept. If you don't accept, you don't go forward.'*

Perceptions of and reactions to aphasia

Relatives' perceptions of aphasia were accurate and specific, grounded in their day-to-day experience. In contrast, those working in nursing homes, none of whom had received any training about communication difficulties, seemed unclear about the nature of aphasia. One nurse thought that Anthea was able to write letters because she saw her scribbling in a notebook. In fact she was copying lists of words.

Everyone generated their own theories about the cause and nature of changes in communication, attributing them to memory loss, to half the larynx not working, and to the brain being asleep. Some people developed elaborate systems for trying to train the person with aphasia and re-establish their skills. Carers tried to get the person to make sounds in order to build these up to make a word. One nurse made the person try to sing the elusive word; as previously mentioned, another insisted that the person try to repeat the name of every item of food and drink before receiving it. Carers stressed how establishing strong routines helped to circumvent communication breakdown:

> *'He's no trouble. He's just so much of a loner. He does the same thing every day. We know his likes and his dislikes. It's hard for a new person to get to know what Fred wants.'*

However formal and informal carers reported that communication often broke down, and this caused frustration, anger and even violence on occasions.

The impact of aphasia and stroke

Relatives talked about the relative impact of aphasia and the physical impairments resulting from stroke. Most were clear that loss of communication, while invisible, was a profound blow to their relationship:

> *'I've lost my husband. I've lost my marriage. All the intimate chit-chat, the gossip. I think it's a disability with a great big capital D.'*

Most people were sensitive to the pain of their partners' losses, and to the frustration of not being able to continue with long-established activities such as gardening, DIY and car maintenance. Many partners also listed their own losses (of lifestyle, freedom, friends, aspirations, financial security and independence), as well as those of the person with aphasia:

> *'It's all very well to dwell on what he has lost, but you lose it by proxy. You're almost disabled by proxy. You have to suffer all the lack of access that the disabled person has to suffer if you're with them.'*

While some people were able to get through each day cheerfully, particularly those with strong routines and a good support network and regular breaks timetabled in, others found the need for their constant presence very constraining. Those whose relationships had been turbulent prior to the stroke found themselves struggling to reconcile complicated and contradictory feelings.

Financial worries were a common experience, particularly for those who had given up work to look after their partner. Only two or three people in the study classed themselves as comfortably off, with no financial problems. The rest found themselves having to economise in order to make ends meet. They bought clothes from charity shops and catalogues, shopped in the economy supermarkets and did without holidays and treats. Those who opted to carry on working did not have the financial pressures but often felt guilty about being out all day and became unwilling to pursue any kind of social life after work.

However of more concern was the social constriction and isolation that descended on the person with aphasia. It was commonly observed that friends had fallen away after an initial show of support. A common explanation was that the friends did not know how to react and what to do when faced with someone who could not speak. Carers were critical of the different approaches adopted: those who teased or chastised their partners were as unpopular as those who talked about, rather than directly to, the person with aphasia. Such distancing was not confined to personal relationships: health and social care workers were perceived as being equally at a loss.

Family members referred to their worries about the future: '*the long, vast years ahead*'. All were concerned about their ability to carry on caring, physically and emotionally, for their partners. Looking ahead to years of hard, physical work, boredom, poverty, isolation, lack of freedom and depression, some discussed the possibility of residential or nursing care. For the older respondents, there was the very real possibility that they would die first or be unable to carry on because of their own illness or disability. Everyone contemplated this with dread:

> '*The main thing I would feel is
> vulnerability for Jean, because the
> thought of what happens if this set-up
> degenerates or breaks up, I don't like to
> contemplate. Some of the conditions
> I've heard about in those places are
> absolutely... don't bear thinking about.*'

Particularly anxious about the future were those who knew how crucially important they were as a kind of intermediary between the person with aphasia and the outside world. Wendy was a good example of this: she felt very concerned lest she should die before Roger, as she knew people would not know how to behave towards him. To that end she worked very hard setting up social networks for Roger – for example, at the bowls club – and by demonstrating her own easy, natural and inclusive forms of interaction.

This example demonstrates the positive and creative approach taken by a number of carers. Despite all the worries, they were able to take pleasure in their relationship. This was hard for those whose relationships had been troubled before, and those who had come to see their partner as a burden, a child, a victim or a drain on their own life, energy and resources. Keeping respect, rather than pity or resentment, as the basis of the relationship seemed to enable relatives to ride the ups and downs, the day-to-day struggles and frustrations, and to balance their own needs with those of everyone else:

> '*We've got a really strong bond, enough
> for me to feel that I could and I can put
> myself in his position. You have to do
> that constantly to understand and to...
> trying to think of ways round things.*'

In these interviews relatives described the complex, shifting patterns of their lives as they looked back, dealt with the present and anticipated the future. They were able to talk about the changes, difficulties, worries and pleasures of day-to-day life. The very process of talking prompted some to reflect on the privilege of language:

> '*I can get it all off my chest, but he can't.*'

Findings from the survey of those providing services for people with severe aphasia

Response rates

The survey was designed to find out 'what happens' to people who have severe aphasia by making contact with the people most likely to come across them in the course of their work: speech and language therapists, support organisers and volunteers, organisations of disabled people and aphasia self-help groups. Of the 506 questionnaires sent out, 151 were returned (30%). These responses can be broken down as follows:

- Speech language therapists (SLTs): 270 questionnaires sent, 94 completed (35%)

- Dysphasia Support (DS): 171 question-naires sent, 32 completed (19%)

- Disabled peoples' organisations (DPO): 48 questionnaires sent, 9 completed (19%)

- Self-help groups (SHG): 21 questionnaires sent, 16 completed (76%).

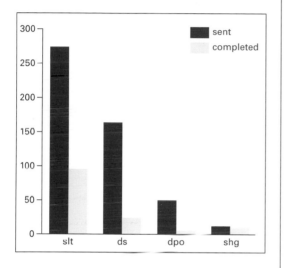

Aphasia self-help groups had the highest rate of return. It seems likely that this was thanks to the efforts of two advisory panel members (Alan Hewitt and Cressida Laywood) in making the questionnaire for self-help groups both relevant and accessible.

While the low response rate from other respondents was perhaps disappointing, it should be understood that the questionnaire they received was long and demanded a considerable amount of time, thought and effort to complete. In addition, it often asked for information to which many respondents did not have access. Given the pressure on resources described by many of the respondents, the low response rate is perhaps not surprising. Nevertheless, those who did respond offered some useful information about the situation of and services for people with severe aphasia across the UK. While it cannot be claimed that the responses are representative of the population as a whole, nevertheless the data provide useful indicators of some of the issues faced by people with severe aphasia across the UK.

The low return rate makes it difficult to formulate any definitive and statistically robust statements about what befalls people who struggle to communicate. Nevertheless, the data raise some interesting questions and concerns regarding the nature of the difficulties faced by this group, their access to and exclusion from services, the nature and timing of the services they are offered, and the issue of liaison and contact between the providers of different health, welfare, support and information services. These topics will be summarised in the following section.

The barriers faced by people with severe aphasia

Our respondents expressed the opinion that people with severe aphasia face major barriers in every aspect of their lives. They perceived people with severe aphasia as being isolated, bored, depressed, socially excluded, misunderstood and not valued by society. Our respondents expressed the desire to improve this situation.

Access to services

The survey data raise a question as to whether all people with severe aphasia have equitable access to services. This arises from the figures given on numbers of clients with severe aphasia, which fall short of the likely prevalence of severe chronic disability following stroke within different populations (Code, 2000). There may also be a concern around the access to services of people from ethnic minority groups, some of whom have a high incidence of diabetes, hypertension and stroke and yet who seem to be sparsely represented in the figures. This accords with current initiatives in stroke service planning, where the importance of developing services that respond to the needs of different populations, including minority ethnic communities, is being emphasised (see, for example, standard two and service model 5.33 in the National Service Framework for Older People, published by the Department of Health (2001)).

The issue of access was developed further by the small number of respondents who expressed concern about the communication accessibility of their services. They raised the issue that people with severe aphasia might have difficulties hearing and enquiring about services, dealing with information about services, negotiating with receptionists, understanding what is offered and dealing with the practical arrangements for taking up a service. In particular, the organisations of disabled people that took part in the survey seemed to have little knowledge and little experience of people with severe aphasia and had difficulty knowing how to make their service accessible to people who struggle to talk, understand, read and write.

Exclusion from services

In addition, it seems that some services effectively exclude people with severe aphasia. Reasons for exclusion appear to be linked to lack of resources, but also concern the nature of the client's response to services and the nature and focus of the service offered. Thus people who are perceived as unmotivated or unco-operative may have a service withdrawn or withheld. Those who have 'reached their potential' in terms of recovery may find that services are discontinued. This suggests that the focus of therapy may fall on making gains in language (which may be unattainable for this group). In some cases respondents made it clear that people who are unlikely to make much recovery are a low priority in the planning of resource-limited services.

While some respondents suggested that clients with severe aphasia did not always fit their services, others turned this on its head and expressed the opinion that their services were unsuitable for this group and this might lead to clients with severe aphasia leaving or withdrawing. Thus large, noisy groups, an emphasis on conversation and predominantly 'pen and paper' activities may cause people with severe aphasia to drop out, as these are not perceived as appropriate to their abilities.

A small number of respondents are making efforts to include people with severe aphasia in the planning, running and auditing of their services. Including people with severe aphasia in such processes demands a tremendous amount of work, time, and preparation of supporting materials (Pound *et al*, 2000). It is hardly surprising, then, that the level of involvement described by the hard-pressed therapists and support workers who responded to this survey seems somewhat limited. Aphasia self-help groups also find it difficult to involve people with severe aphasia in contributing to the running of their groups, other than in activities such as washing up and making tea. This is not surprising, and probably influences the desire expressed for more support and input from therapists. People with severe aphasia may be excluded from contributing at this level because the support they need to enable them to contribute is not available and because inclusion may not be seen as a priority.

Long term support for people with severe aphasia

Most of those who responded to the survey expressed the view that long-term support is desirable for people who are living with an intractable impairment. Yet many respondents voiced frustration at the short-term nature of their own services, even though information and advice is usually available to clients and their families on an on-going basis. In particular it was felt that speech and language therapy should be ongoing, although often the form this should take was not specified. This desire to support people with severe aphasia on a more long-term basis accords with the fact that many respondents were highly aware of wide-ranging and intractable obstacles faced by people living with severe communication difficulties.

Liaison between health and other services

The survey also highlighted a possible lack of liaison between the voluntary and therapeutic services and community-based health, education and welfare services that might be useful to people with severe aphasia. The respondents expressed the need for training and education of all professionals in severe aphasia, and for integration of therapy and community services. Yet, according to their responses, there seems to be little systematic contact between, say, therapy services and social services and respite, welfare and information services in the community. The survey findings give the impression of effective multi-disciplinary teamwork within healthcare settings, and usually good liaison between therapeutic and voluntary services concerned with stroke (although many voluntary sector respondents indicated that they wished for more guidance and input from therapists). But there seems to be little contact with people providing other services that could prove useful to people with severe aphasia, such as adult educators, employment advisors, day care and respite agencies. This corresponds with the findings from the ethnographic study, in which little liaison between services was evident.

With the exception of the organisations of disabled people, our respondents were largely concerned with the provision of speech and language therapy, perceived as the most important service for this group. Relatively little attention was paid to other potentially useful services.

Respondents were very aware of the difficulties and obstacles facing this group. Public ignorance and disrespect were perceived as particularly important. However it seems that therapy services in particular may lose touch with people who have severe aphasia as the years pass, and may be unaware of the domestic situation, even of those with whom they are in contact. The need for long-term involvement and support, counselling, carer support, and training for all professionals, service providers and advocates was seen to be essential. Yet who is to do this, as an oft-cited problem seems to be a lack of resources? There are not enough people and there is too little time.

Some respondents expressed the need to take stock and review priorities in planning both the nature and timing of therapeutic intervention for this group. One suggestion made was that therapy for people with severe aphasia should focus on training diverse service providers and advocates, integration with other services in the community, and advice and support. This might mean that a relatively short-term input could bring about long-term impacts; a concept that may well be appealing to the hard-pressed therapists and support workers. However, it would represent a change and a challenge for services that have largely focused on trying to bring about improvements in the language and communication of people with aphasia.

The people who took the time to respond to this survey are arguably concerned about people with severe aphasia and are motivated to improve their lot. They also have considerable knowledge, expertise and experience concerning aphasia. If an (albeit small) proportion of such skilled, motivated, experienced service providers feel that aspects of their service are inaccessible, inappropriate and exclusionary, this raises questions about other services where the providers may have little knowledge or experience of severe aphasia and the obstacles faced by those who live with it. Some therapists, support workers and aphasia self-help groups have plenty of ideas about how they could make their services more appropriate, inclusive and accessible (for example, using supported conversation techniques, adapting information and signage, developing appropriate activities, training carers, professionals and ancillary workers). But what about the services that have no training, knowledge or experience? As one respondent from the disabled people's organisation put it: '*As we have no contact with this group, we can probably assume they are having difficulties in using the service.*'

This suggests that services themselves, rather than people with severe aphasia, may be 'hard to reach'.

Chapter Four

What happens to people with severe aphasia? tracking the process of social exclusion

This study set out to explore what happens to people with severe aphasia. Twenty people with marked communication difficulties following stroke agreed to take part in the project. Over a period of about eight months I visited each person in a variety of settings, watching, documenting and, when appropriate, taking part in whatever was going on. While the initial focus was on the people with aphasia, this widened as the project unfolded. Partners, families, friends and service providers became an inevitable part of the study, as did the various contexts, domestic and institutional, in which myriad interactions took place. A detailed documentation of different everyday settings, verbal and non-verbal exchanges, routines, rituals and artefacts was gradually built up. From these details it was possible to capture some sense of what happens to people with severe aphasia in their everyday lives, to examine the nature of institutional practice and culture, and to trace the subtle and not so subtle processes whereby people with severe aphasia are socially excluded or included. These microcosmic data were supplemented with interviews with family members and paid carers, together with information from a survey of speech and language therapists, voluntary organisations, groups of disabled people and aphasia self-help initiatives across the UK.

What is social exclusion?

The government definition of social exclusion refers to: '… what can happen when people or areas suffer from a combination of linked problems, such as unemployment, poor skills, low incomes, poor housing, high crime environments, bad health and family breakdown' (www.socialexclusionunit.gov.uk/seu). This definition acknowledges the complicated interconnection of factors that bring about exclusion. Some definitions take a wider view. People are thought to be excluded when they are not part of the networks that support most people in ordinary life – of family, friends, community and employment. Among many others, people in poverty, ex-prisoners, homeless people, people with AIDS, people with learning disabilities and people with mental health problems might all be said to be at risk of exclusion. Thus exclusion is a very broad concept: it includes not only deprivation but also problems of social relationships, including stigma, social isolation and failures in social protection.

This chapter teases out some of the indicators of social exclusion (and inclusion) and considers them with reference to the day-to-day experiences of people with severe aphasia. The data will be considered in terms of three domains in which social exclusion is evident: the social infrastructure, social relations and personal response and attitude. This is not to say that there are clear-cut boundaries between these domains. Each influences and affects the others. For example, how a therapist or care attendant behaves may be affected by resource and infrastructural issues and may also impact on the confidence levels and self-esteem of a person with aphasia. Throughout this study, the complicated impacts of living with loss of language have become increasingly apparent.

Applying some of these concepts to the situations described in this study, it becomes possible to track the processes of social exclusion for this group of people, to look at some contributing factors, and to start thinking about how such processes might be countered.

Work, money and services: infrastructural aspects of the social exclusion of people with severe aphasia

Exclusion can arise from the actions of those institutions contributing to and constructing societal infrastructure. The Library and Information Commission (www.lic.gov.uk/publications/policyreports/inclusion) states that key issues within this domain include access to resources and services (health, housing, education, employment, transport), the relative quality of service provision, and access to communications media, information and communication technology and information. The Commission also describes how the impact of the geographical location of resources, the 'tyranny of distance and the nature of the place' can all lead to exclusion. Do people with aphasia experience exclusion in these contexts?

Work

A review of the field notes quickly demonstrates that social exclusion is a common experience for people affected by severe aphasia. Even within this relatively small group there was plenty of experience of major restrictions: return to work was usually impossible. The youngest participant, Ruth, was the only person in the group of 20 people who was working in any way. This was as a cleaner, an occupation much at odds with her aspirations to train as a teacher or a nurse. Another young participant, Tom, was still hoping that recovery would enable him to return to work as a self-employed contract electrician, and to resume his previous lifestyle, travelling nationally and internationally to work on various building schemes. However the likelihood of this seemed remote, given his limited language and the epilepsy and physical restrictions that had started with the stroke. He had no access to any opportunity for re-entering the workplace. Long-standing problems with national insurance payments consolidated the financial difficulties facing Tom and his partner Jacqui (she had stopped work to look after him). Most days he lay in bed until noon, then watched tv through the afternoon and evening, lying on the sofa with a cigarette in one hand and the remote control in the other. Constantly spending time together was starting to have a negative effect on the couple, with the result that their relationship was placed under severe strain.

Terry, a cabinet-maker, had tried to return to work some weeks after his stroke, full-time and with no modifications in his working conditions or hours. He had quickly become ill and exhausted and had had to abandon his efforts. His workshop at home was still orderly, with the tools laid out in neat rows. During one visit he wrote the word 'jops' and then said '*All gone*', with a sorrowful expression. Like many of the other participants who had been working, he seemed to regret not just the loss of income but also the major change of lifestyle and identity that stroke had brought. His wife had to work full-time in order to make ends meet. Gill frequently referred to her work as a hairdresser and seemed to express through her gestures and facial expression her regret that she no longer enjoyed the status and pleasure of working in a skilled job. Mary also expressed her sense of loss of influence and power, comparing activity, travel, prestige and excitement with the boredom and restriction of her current existence. Her situation was highlighted by the fact that she still lived in a commuter suburb, where there seemed to be little evidence of community life, at least during the working week. She passed her time mostly at home, alone. Those, like Donald, who had retired from paid employment, indicated that they missed engagement in the voluntary and community work they had once enjoyed.

Making ends meet

With a few exceptions, people who took part in this study were experiencing financial hardship. Relatives described shopping from charity shops and catalogues, foregoing holidays, and '*robbing Peter to pay Paul*'. In many cases, families with two incomes were reduced to relying on benefits (the partner having also given up work to care for the person affected by the stroke). The welfare and benefit systems seemed inhospitable. Access to benefits, information and support was unpredictable. The struggle for benefits had taken their toll, particularly in the early days when the chaos and uncertainty of acute illness were compounded by worry and hardship. A few years post-stroke, some people were well supported and organised and had enough to live comfortably. Others were still economising, with little prospect of things improving.

Housing

Five of the 20 people who took part in the project lived in poor or inadequate housing. They were experiencing significant problems with the house itself (damp, cold, dereliction, noise), and were also worried about crime in their locality. Rates of street crime and burglary in these places were high. One carer described having been mugged, and I personally witnessed an aggressive verbal assault on Gill and her husband in the car park of a supermarket.

Of course, the financial and housing hardships and employment worries experienced by the participants are not solely related to aphasia. Other factors, such as mobility difficulties, fatigue and epilepsy, also had an effect on the person's ability to resume work and restore previous levels of income. However, difficulty communicating, as well as being a major barrier to effective functioning in all but menial work settings, meant that negotiation, discussion of alternative courses of action and access to new or different training were also barred. This meant that tasks that might previously have been shared (for example, asking the authorities to consider a change of council flat) fell to the person who could talk and write. Although some people tried to ensure their partners were involved in decisions, in practice this was often very difficult.

Services

Access to services seemed patchy and inequitable. Most people had input from support services such as home care, enabling them to continue living at home, but only one couple had found funding from the Independent Living Foundation, ensuring continuous, high quality care. Some people, years after their stroke, were continuing to receive physiotherapy and occupational and speech and language therapy. Others had no continuing input. Often it was clear that the person with aphasia would have benefited from a particular health or social care service that was not available or accessible. For example, Christine was living in constant pain, her right arm swollen and difficult to move. Yet she had no access to a physiotherapist. She could not ask for this herself and had to rely on her husband, who had health worries of his own, to raise her predicament in his own consultations, to little effect.

Tom and Ruth were both facing major changes and needed support in considering their future plans, input from an employment advisor and perhaps opportunities for accessing alternative training and sources of income. These opportunities were not available or accessible. Another need was for support in dealing with communication breakdown. I witnessed episodes of frustration and tension within families and institutions. Some family members described moments of aggression, and even violence, when a message could not be expressed or understood. Yet none could recall having received guidance on how to make communication easier and deal with problems when things went wrong. Wendy spoke for many when she said she acted on instinct when trying to help Roger during his frequent struggles with communication.

The issue of access to services was prominent in the survey, a number of service provider respondents indicating that their services for people with aphasia were not accessible to those with severe difficulties. Sometimes this was because information about the service was not understood, and sometimes because the service itself was unsuitable: for example, it focused on pencil and paper activities. This perception was supported in the ethnographic study. In day centres and in volunteer-led groups, I watched people with severe communication problems sitting through question-and-

answer games. These seemed clearly inappropriate. However, despite being unable to join in, some people with aphasia clearly enjoyed the social aspect of activities such as quizzes and bingo.

Some services seemed irrelevant to the needs or concerns of the person with aphasia. For example, Tom spent occupational therapy sessions sanding a member of staff's garden furniture and painting wooden toys. His perceived 'lack of motivation' in these activities meant that he was going to be discharged soon, and that would be the end of any form of treatment or support. Ruth reluctantly joined in with quizzes and arts and crafts at her day centre. She commented that her daughter would enjoy such activities, but they were not relevant to her own situation. Her profound dislike of the day centre was clear: '*I bloody hate it.*'

In some cases, services that were provided clearly missed the mark. At one day centre a worker had spent a considerable amount of time making a wooden communication aid for David. He could not use it. It was unwieldy, awkward to handle (he had a right-sided paralysis) and displayed confusing words and images that he could not understand and that were not relevant to him. In addition, the assistant was trying to teach him to use Amerind, a form of sign language. She had little training and no input from anyone with knowledge of aphasia or communication aid technology, yet she had been given special responsibility for supporting people with communication difficulties. The time and effort invested in these attempts to help communication were effectively wasted. Another example of wasted resources concerned Charles, who was experiencing difficulties negotiating the precipitous, open-plan stairs in his home. Charles was restricted to sitting, eating, sleeping, washing and using the commode in one small room. The therapist had not visited the home to see his situation for herself. He could not describe his difficulties to her. She felt that Charles was not motivated and that her advice went 'in one ear and out the other'.

The quality of services such as these seemed severely compromised by a lack of integration: between the real-life issues faced and the activities of day centres and rehabilitation units and between service providers with different expertise and skills (for example, day centre or nursing home staff working with people with aphasia on a daily basis commented that they had no contact with speech and language therapists). These issues were also highlighted in the survey. People with severe communication difficulties were commonly described by service providers as 'hard to reach', but perhaps this description should be applied to the services themselves?

Information

Information and explanation enhance access to services. People with language and communication difficulties need information to be adapted so that it is easier to understand. Yet a number of observations suggest that little or no account is taken of aphasia by providers of health or social care, voluntary or public services. I rarely saw people with aphasia being given any information about the activities in which they were involved. There was no explanation of rationale, benefits or limitations, and no choice. The explanations I did witness were often loaded with jargon and difficult to understand. People who perhaps didn't understand were considered 'unmotivated'. Inaccessible information was also evident in written communications. Mary asked me to explain an official letter she had received about recommencing driving. It was expressed in formal language, and was difficult to understand. No account had been taken of her language difficulties.

Clear, accessible written and spoken information about services is now a statutory right under the *Disability Discrimination Act (1995)*. Yet it seems that some providers of health, social care and other services may have little concept of the possible restrictions faced by someone who struggles to talk, write, read and understand. A number of respondents in the survey described the information about their services as inaccessible. Clearly, there are resource issues here. Training is needed to convey the nature of aphasia and ways of enhancing spoken and written communication so that equality and access issues are understood and services of all kinds can be delivered effectively. Another infrastructural problem concerns time as a resource. Many workers in rehabilitation units, day centres and nursing homes described their full workloads and rapid pace of work. Not only had they had no training; it seemed unlikely that they would be able to fit into their schedules the labour-intensive process of adapting written and spoken information. Again, these issues accord with points raised in the survey.

Training

According to people working in the different service contexts, methods of communicating and different techniques for 'managing' were mostly transmitted informally, passed on from one worker to another. For example, in Anthea's nursing home more experienced people worked alongside newcomers to pass on their skills and tips for managing Anthea's day-to-day care and avoiding trouble with her. Idiosyncratic theories and ways of working often developed unchecked, as in the case of David's care-worker and the communication aid. Fred's keyworker, for example, made him repeat the names of items of food or drink before she gave them to him, convinced that this was good for him. Within these service contexts, I saw no evidence of anyone using any methods for supporting communication. A number of people in residential and social services settings commented that they had no training in communication. A staff nurse in Brenda's nursing home observed that training priorities were crisis management techniques and the physical handling of patients.

Despite many examples of communication breakdown, there seemed little evidence of questioning and concern about their skills and practice on the part of service providers. Therapists, day centre staff, volunteer helpers, nursing home attendants and respite staff often seemed confident about what they were doing and how they were doing it. The underpinning rationale for a service was embedded in the culture of the various institutions and often went unarticulated and unquestioned. Although some respondents in the survey aired concerns about their services for people with severe aphasia, they were in a minority.

In some cases professional confidence was overwhelming, manifested in an authoritative style of communication, extensive use of expert jargon, and continuous directed activity. Rather than viewing this critically in terms of individual practice, it would perhaps be fairer to think in terms of infrastructural constraints, pressures and culture. Lack of training is clearly an issue here, for workers at every level in the different care professions. This ethnographic study exposed the multiple, contested meanings that different people bring to aphasia.

Information and communication technology (ICT)

Access to ICT was very limited for the group taking part in the study. Only Terry and Roger had access to home computers. Wendy described how she was carefully encouraging and helping Roger to develop his skills, building on activities he could achieve: for example, printing out digital photographs or placing files into folders that she had created. She dedicated a lot of time to supporting Roger in this way. Terry spent one day a week in the computer suite at the day centre (using it to try to re-train his speech). The time and support he needed were simply not available. The worker who was helping clients with the computers could only spend a few minutes with him and he talked and acted very quickly. Setting up Terry's activities so fast, he inadvertently ensured that Terry would constantly need to return to him for help. At home Terry was using the computer for entertainment and his wife, who worked full time, found his constant requests for help an added drain on her energy. Again, access to ICT for people with major communication problems requires dedicated time – a resource that seems in short supply.

Geography and 'the nature of the place'

There was some evidence of difficulty with geographical location of services in the study. In the survey, transport problems were identified as a major obstacle to the uptake of services, particularly in rural areas. The small scale ethnographic study showed how much time people spent travelling to or from services, or waiting to be picked up, even in an urban setting. Those who were able to do so negotiated lifts from friends and neighbours. For Tom, the long wait for the ambulance extended his morning in the occupational therapy workshop by several hours. Others waited sometimes for hours to be picked up or dropped back home, in the company of people from the same area. So Terry regularly travelled home from the day centre in a large bright blue bus, together with a group of elderly people with learning difficulties. For Charles, the wait for transport to the day centre took on particular urgency, as he would rather use the toilet there than the commode in his front room at home.

Lack of respect and value often seemed to be embodied in environments that contrasted with peoples' home settings. Some institutional environments were shabby, poorly cared for, with broken equipment and un-watered plants (a point made by Anthea's visitors in her notebook). In some cases the geography of the setting, the way in which space was organised and used, consolidated isolation and exclusion. Albert sat for hours in the small alcove off the main room, silent, in contact with no one, the tv murmuring in the corner. His solitude was accompanied by continuous background noise: the amplified office phone ringing constantly, often unanswered; music; the crash of equipment from the kitchen and the staff calling back and forth to each other. Frank and Terry's respite care settings were hospital-like, with lots of clinical equipment. But they were also shabby, with ill-fitting curtains, dirty walls, un-watered plants, tv and radio broken, no remote control.

In these details, institutional environments often seemed to express the value and esteem, or lack of it, with which clients were regarded. Even table-settings demonstrated this. At Fred's home the table was set with knives and forks, mats, napkins, salt and pepper, jugs of water and glasses, fresh flowers. At Brenda's private nursing home, soup was served out in plastic bowls, and economy lemonade dispensed from big bottles. There was no salt and pepper on the tables, and no napkins or jugs of water. Often the reality of the institutional environments was at odds with the rhetoric of publicity material. The brochure for Brenda's home described the use of fresh produce at every meal, yet she was eating catering pack soup, fish, chips and frozen peas and tinned mandarin oranges with evaporated milk. In Albert's case, the brochure described an inclusive and friendly atmosphere that was not apparent during my visits.

Notice boards were particularly revealing, as they expressed aspects of staff attitudes towards service users in a direct, unmediated fashion. At Pete's respite centre, authoritarian instructions were pinned on every wall. A notice on his door conveyed stark details of Fred's physical needs and methods of 'handling' him. Strikingly, there were no equivalent instructions concerning communication. The way in which the notice was phrased demonstrated how Fred had been depersonalised:

'Movement in bed: independent. In/out bed: assistance to sit. On/off chair: independent. On/off toilet: independent. Assistance with trousers. No of carers: 1. In/out bath. Parler bath. Standing/walking: n/a. Sitting: independent. In/out car/vehicle: balance and legs and feet. Build: medium. Height: medium. History of falls: none. Traffic light: red. Unable to verbally communicate but is very aware of needs. CVA has caused left side paralysis. Hoist due to CVA problem.'

Interpersonal exclusion

Social exclusion can also be manifested in another domain: interpersonal communication and behaviour. Social exclusion can result from association or lack of association with groups and places in society: family; neighbours; friends; workmates; people of similar age or gender or culture or religion; disabled people. People can feel excluded because they are no longer part of a group to which they once belonged, or because they belong to a group that they have always perceived as being excluded.

Close personal relationships

There was much evidence of interpersonal exclusion within the small group of people who took part in the study. While couples and families generally held together (although not without tensions and difficulties), many relatives described how friends and workmates had fallen away because they did not know how to communicate and seemed to feel awkward and even frightened. Some interlocutors developed strategies that were also profoundly excluding: issuing a string of single word commands; talking about rather than to the person; teasing; insisting on words and phrases being repeated, or simply not acknowledging the person. Wendy's descriptions of awkward conversations with friends and family indicate how common such strategies were, and the ways in which she tried to deal with them:

> 'One chap came, he did come a couple of times, but they seemed to sort of, they bossed Rog about and I hated that. "Now come along, I'm sure you could say more than that," and I wanted to slap them quite honestly and I'm not a violent person and I just felt, I wanted with this particular person I wanted him to go anyway because I think he thought the best answer for Rog was for him to be assertive and for him to say: "Oh come on Rog, you can do better than that, you can say this and you can say that," and I hated it when people told him what he could say and what he couldn't say, I felt as if he was being bullied. He said: "I'm not going to visit him if he's going to come out with any of that Spanish or that Portuguese he keeps trying to talk," you see? And I thought: "Well I don't want you to come now," and he said: "Don't you forget, mind, you tell him I don't want to have to listen to any of that rubbish he was saying."

> 'They'd both be stood in the kitchen telling me all these tales and I'd say: "Well why are you telling me?" I said: "Why don't you just go in and tell your dad?" but they felt awkward. I said: "Look, ok, he can't answer you back, he can't respond in the way you're used to, but he understands everything you're saying." I said: "Go in

the room and have this conversation with your father," and I used to have to tell them to do that, and the times I had to point that out.'

Of course, not everyone in the study had an advocate like Wendy working to make sure they were included. Some, like Gill, would confront and challenge such behaviours but others chose to withdraw from contact. Jean was very reluctant to leave the house, even to go on an outing with her husband. He felt she was frightened and expressed his own frustration at being cooped up. Mary rarely saw people and spent many hours sitting alone. No one visited Tom, and his only social contact was for one or two hours a week down at the pub. Thanks to close circuit security tv, Christine was able to watch her friends from the block of flats coming in the main entrance and riding in the lift. This was the sum of their contact. Generally, people with aphasia lost contacts that they had enjoyed through sporting or other interests. Roger's golfing friends never called round now. Jean's only visitors were her daughter and granddaughter. Everyone in the study seemed to experience some social constriction: a narrowing of social contact that contrasted with life before the stroke.

There is no doubt that other factors such as physical impairment and financial problems also contributed to difficulties maintaining personal relationships. I saw for myself how hard it was for Tom and Jacqui to visit the local pub. In bitterly cold weather, they took over an hour to cover a route they had previously walked in ten minutes. They couldn't afford a taxi and had to face the prospect of the return journey being even longer and more effortful because it was uphill. Jacqui pointed out that the lifts were quite often broken, so Tom would have to end his outing by climbing up seven flights of stairs. The physical effort of getting out was sometimes overwhelming.

However, some exceptional episodes showed the potential for social inclusion and cohesion as people with aphasia entered new social groups or were absorbed into communities. Miss Silver seemed to enjoy the church service held at her day centre: an event that attracted many people from her local community and gave her a chance to catch up with old friends and acquaintances. Wendy had spent months encouraging Roger's forays into the bowling club. She had joined too and accompanied him to every game for nearly a year. He was now able to attend matches on his own, and his team mates were looking out for him and had learned about aphasia and ways of communicating. Mrs Fell organised a weekly visit from Donald's friends from church and the choral society. They followed a strict routine, staying for only one hour and trying out a few minutes of singing exercises with Donald. The social inclusion of Roger and Donald in this way had demanded a lot of careful work and attention on the part of their wives. Wendy thought deeply about how people communicated with Roger, and would often demonstrate how to involve him in the conversation. David's wife was also very skilled at maintaining natural, flowing conversation and modelling that for people who visited. The skilled, sensitive support offered by these people exacerbated their concerns about what would happen were they to become ill, or to die before the person with aphasia.

Relationships with service providers

Although social attachments based on friendship or work or interest diminished or changed for people with aphasia, everyone in the study entered into new relationships with providers of health and social care and voluntary services. Everyone became the recipient of some service: as a client of a day centre, a patient in a respite setting, a resident in a nursing home, a recipient of therapy or a member of a stroke club. Within these settings, as within families and partnerships, other peoples' attitudes and the quality of their communication varied. In some cases service providers were attentive, respectful and able to communicate in a way that both supported and included the silent person without marking them out as different or an object of pity. The attendant at Fred's nursing home, for example, chatted to the residents in a friendly, natural way as she served their meals. She sat down with them until they had finished and she could remove their plates. She offered residents choice and support and eased their vulnerabilities and difficulties with gentle humour. The woman who visited Ivy to do her hair and to help her at home was able to engage her in a long conversation about her family, even though Ivy could not say a word. As pointed out previously, such examples of successful and respectful communication seemed to be a matter of individual style and instinct, rather than a result of training.

But at every level there were also examples of lack of respect and poor communication. Sometimes these had potentially serious consequences. Frank's respite care team only discovered by chance that he had swallowing problems and needed a specially modified diet to minimise the possibility of choking. They did not know how to communicate with him, not having read the notes his wife had sent, and it was a matter of trial and error as to whether he got his message across. Charles could not let his therapist know about his significant problems with mobility at home; she did not try to find out and chastised him for not practising his therapy exercises. Pete struggled without success to convey some information to the manager of the day centre.

Strategies for managing the communication difficulties varied. Albert's nursing assistant addressed him using single and two word commands ('Come on. Back.')

45

before dragging him backwards on a dining chair across the lounge towards the table for lunch. In Pete's case, the manager made little attempt to understand what he was trying to convey, and within a couple of minutes she had left him in the corridor, saying she would phone his wife and ask her.

Sometimes people with communication problems were teased or treated in other disrespectful ways. People working at Anthea's nursing home laughingly imitated her idiosyncratic way of speaking as they walked away from her room. One nurse repeatedly stuck out her tongue at Brenda. The physio told Charles she would show him some 'pretty pictures'. People with aphasia were told to 'behave'. Sometimes people were patronised. Gill was patted on the arm and spoken to in a slow, sing-song voice. David had to sit silently as stroke club volunteers said of him: '*He's got a lovely wife.*' People became invisible, talked about as if they were not there.

Relationships with service users

Perhaps unsurprisingly, Pete did not enjoy his trips to the day centre, and expressed this with sighs and a weary facial expression. He seemed an unwilling member of a new social group. Ruth, who had more language, also expressed her distaste at the thought of going to the day centre. For her, the place marked out her vulnerabilities, a person who was impaired: '*I bloody hate it. I just want to be right.*' She had little to do with the other clients, most of whom had physical and cognitive impairments. She preferred instead to talk to staff and students, many of whom were similar to her in age and background. She consolidated her distance from the other clients by busying herself with tasks around the centre: laying tables and removing plates. She didn't want to eat with the group and sat away from the tables while other clients dined. Although she acknowledged the

profoundly serious nature of her difficulties with communication, Ruth saw herself being in this situation on a temporary basis.

Ruth's aphasia was the major long-standing consequence of her haemorrhage. Her physical problems had mostly resolved. But her word-finding difficulties and her problems taking in complex written or spoken information meant that her career plans were jeopardised and her sense of herself severely altered. Yet her troubles were invisible, and often not evident to others until she spoke. She was acutely aware of being different, not being right. She was unable to revisit her plans and unwilling to enter new communities until things improved for her. She was similar to Terry, whose wife described how he had become increasingly isolated and reluctant to venture out because of other people's reactions to him:

> '*And how, well that's how he explained how their attitude was and that as he'd go by, talking about him or that's how he'd, or they'd, if he was going up to them they'd go another direction. I mean he still gets this stuff now up at the shops, if he sees somebody he used to work with he'll look at them and they'll walk away, they can't cope with it you know, they walk away... He doesn't go out as much as he used to. Yeah, he used to go out a lot more, but he seems to be drawing back, getting more and more isolated as time goes on.*'

Personal aspects of exclusion

> '*Individuals may become excluded through experiencing or perceiving alienation; isolation; lack of identity; low self esteem; passivity; dependence, bewilderment, fear, anger, apathy, low aspirations and hope-lessness.*' (Library and Information Commission. www.lic.gov.uk)

It would be wrong to suggest that everyone in the study experienced such feelings or displayed these features all the time. Although it is hard to get beneath superficial comments on this issue, some, like Ivy and Christine, seemed to have become accustomed to the changes brought by stroke and to find enjoyment and pleasure in day-to-day things like being with family, eating meals and watching favourite programmes on tv. Harry relished his vegetable plot. Ivy also continued to enjoy going out and travelled with her husband to visit relatives in Italy. Gill, too, seemed to enjoy many aspects of her life: the company of her daughters and husband, drinking in the social club and at home, swimming. Roger clearly adored his wife and family and enjoyed the companionship of the bowling club. Terry loved using the computer, despite the frustrations it brought him. He and his wife took holidays in the Isles of Scilly and he appreciated the peace and beauty of this setting.

Isolation and boredom

But the more personal manifestations of exclusion were also evident. Often these could not be framed or expressed in words. Rather, they were conveyed through facial expression, body language, sighing and vocalisation. Many participants seemed to be isolated. In most cases visitors no longer called, perhaps because they did not know how to react to someone who could no longer communicate. Even in situations in which contact with others was still plentiful, people with aphasia were still effectively isolated by being treated disrespectfully, teased, patronised or ignored. A number of respondents chose to stay put, rather than venturing out. Anthea refused to leave her room at the nursing home, and passed every day with only herself for company. Some people seemed low-spirited and depressed, particularly those who were alone for long stretches of time and who had little to do other than watch television. Boredom also

seemed common. Previous means of entertainment and relaxation, such as reading or doing crosswords, were no longer possible. Access to information and communication technology was limited, and those participants who did spend time with computers needed intensive support. Malfunctioning sets without remote control meant that some people, like Frank and Charles, were unable to watch television in institutional settings. Three people in the study now spent most of each day smoking.

Identity

Although this was often hard to address directly, it was clear that everyone had been forced to face major losses in terms of identity and life plans. Reconfiguration of self, their past and future, seemed hard without language, as there could be little discussion and negotiation of the subtler aspects of change and loss. Many of those who had been working or studying before their stroke found themselves confronting major changes in life plan and a constriction of their aspirations, but with little acknowledgement of this, and no support. Personal histories seemed to be lost, particularly in the case of those participants who were in nursing homes, where no one knew much about them other than the most basic information.

There were many examples throughout the study of participants being treated as if they were not quite a person: being referred to in the third person in their presence; being ignored or talked over; being put off; being given commands. There seems to be a danger that if a person cannot communicate they may be perceived as less than human: their personhood is lost. It is difficult to imagine the impact of this on a person's sense of self. For all but the most robust, such distancing and disengagement must have an eroding impact on identity. Language is a primary means by which we make our personhood known. For Wendy this was a critical issue, although difficult to capture in words. She found she could deal better with moments of tension or difficulty when she identified with Roger and put herself in his place, setting his personhood at the centre of her thoughts:

> 'Well I'd say the most important thing is what I've been saying all along, you really, you have, I mean you have to think about yourself, of course you do, but you really and truly do have to put yourself in a position for you to handle it, for you to, to me it's a way of controlling what's going on between the two of you, to try and put yourself in that person's position. I think it helps you not to get, not to get out of patience with it, how can I explain it?'

It is commonly acknowledged that institutional settings can have a depersonalising effect on clients, patients and residents. In such settings pressure of work means that staff often have to be concerned '*with the mass not the individual*', as a nurse at Brenda's home put it. In such settings, in which large numbers of people are managed, perhaps it is inevitable that individuality is subsumed, even in the case those who can communicate. Aphasia makes it more difficult to apprehend a person's individuality, character, personality and history. People with aphasia who enter institutional settings are particularly vulnerable to being passed over and disregarded.

Frustration and anger

Frustration was a common experience, too. Plenty of people showed their frustration when communication broke down. However, there were only one or two episodes in which anger was displayed: for example, when Terry became exasperated with Martin's attempts to help him use the computer and turned on him to try and make him be quiet. But family members described how communication trouble would commonly spill over into frustration, anger and sometimes violence.

Lack of control

Although some families endeavoured to include the person with aphasia in decisions, the study revealed very little evidence of people with severe aphasia exercising choice and control in their day-to-day lives, other than at the most basic level. The most powerful manifestations of this control were often non-verbal. Donald closed his eyes to shut out other people in the room, sometimes for ten minutes at a time. Anthea would focus her gaze on the pudding she was eating rather than continuing an interaction. Jean kept her eyes fixed on the television rather than turning to greet her visitor.

People with aphasia were often over-ruled and unable to express their opinions or object to what was happening or what other people said. Lack of language rendered many relatively powerless in the face of the verbal strengths of others. Nevertheless, despite the difficulties, one or two people continued to make a point of communicating in a confident way. Gill would often initiate exchanges with other people, using gesture and facial expression, and enquire after the health of a member of their family. Ironically, at one point she was asked to do this by a volunteer driver, as some kind of performance of her communication skills: '*Go on, ask me how my wife is.*' Like Gill, Roger would often persist in his efforts to convey an idea or make an enquiry even when the going was very difficult. But many others would give up, worn out by the effort of trying to convey some point or express an idea, or sometimes embarrassed by the struggle. In addition, those around seemed to have little idea of how to support people with aphasia in getting their message out.

Bewilderment, too, seemed a common experience. Harry could not understand what had happened to his speech and why he was finding things so difficult. Others, like Charles, became bewildered when they could not follow some information or instructions. Yet there was no evidence of any attempt on the part of service providers to make written or spoken instructions or information easier to understand.

Relatives described similar feelings of 'being all at sea' themselves, particularly in the early days following stroke. This highlights an important point. While it is possible to trace the manifestations of social exclusion in the lives of people with aphasia, many relatives and family members also shared aspects of this experience, and found their lives changed and themselves excluded and undermined in similar ways. As Pete's wife put it:

> 'It's all very well to dwell on what he has lost, but you lose it by proxy. You're almost disabled by proxy. You have to suffer all the lack of access that the disabled person has to suffer if you're with them. The lack of freedom, when you could go off and do as you please, but you've got to be there for that person. So your activities are curtailed as well...'

It is possible to identify different but interacting levels of social exclusion in the day-to-day lives of the participants with aphasia: infrastructural, interpersonal and personal or internal. Social exclusion does not seem to be a fixed, immutable state: it varies and changes according to circumstances, particularly in terms of interpersonal processes. So a person with aphasia might be socially excluded one moment, as a situation unfolds, and included the next. One moment a person might effectively engage someone with aphasia in a conversation and the next undermine them with teasing or criticism, a brief, impenetrable comment or a pitying expression. This dynamic was apparent on many occasions in the study. People with aphasia who attended the feedback meetings

reinforced this point, indicating that their sense of exclusion or inclusion varied from situation to situation, and from moment to moment.

What would make a difference to the experience of severe aphasia?

Social exclusion is clearly evident in the details of everyday experience documented in this study. Encouragingly, there are also some examples of social inclusion; people with aphasia can become engaged in meaningful and pleasurable conversations, interactions and activities and be involved in making or sharing decisions. Often the source of exclusion or inclusion lies within other people: how they communicate and attempt to understand; their manner and approach, their resourcefulness and energy; their values. This in turn is embedded in and influenced by the social groups, cultures and institutions within which individuals operate. While it may be easy to identify ways in which, say, a therapist, a residential care attendant, a volunteer supporter, an employer or a family member might improve their communication skills, to focus on these aspects of inclusion alone would over-simplify the issue. It would deny the influence of infrastructure, resources, tradition, relationships, habit and culture. Similarly, feelings of isolation, boredom or depression (the personal aspects of exclusion) cannot be addressed in isolation from the influences that bring them about.

Tackling the social exclusion of people with severe aphasia therefore needs to be a multi-faceted, multi-dimensional process; one that reflects the complicated, mercurial nature of the experience. We have seen that social exclusion is manifest within infrastructural, interpersonal and personal contexts. Within each of these contexts possibilities for bringing about social inclusion hinge on four factors: support for communication; acknowledgment and

49

respect; opportunity and access, and attention to the environment.

Support for communication

In the study, not one person coming into contact with people with aphasia could recall having received training or help on what to do when communication is problematic. Difficulties with communication were experienced across the board, from highly trained professionals to the poorly trained or untrained workers who often have prolonged, day-to-day contact with people with aphasia. In some cases breakdowns in communication were witnessed but not perceived to be problematic by service providers.

It is clear from the study that much could be done to support those who come into contact with people who have aphasia in every context in developing practical skills and creative strategies for recognising and dealing with communication breakdown. Means of supporting communication and conversation are well understood and can be taught (Kagan, 1998). The study makes clear that there is an urgent need to equip those around people with aphasia with these basic skills and strategies so that communication and conversation can be enhanced. These skills should be afforded as much priority as the manual and 'handling' skills that currently seem to be the main focus of training.

Acknowledgement and respect

The study highlighted many subtler forms of discrimination and exclusion: a pitying attitude, a lack of respect, the implication that slow progress is deliberate, the teasing, the delicate undermining of people who cannot speak. Such attitudes can be manifested in body language, gesture, facial expression, turn of phrase and even tone of voice. Consequently they can be extremely difficult to identify and to influence. Mercurial they

may be, but such behaviours are a powerful source and means of exclusion. There is potential for exclusion in every interaction with people at every level of power and influence: family members, friends, rehabilitation experts, tea ladies, benefits personnel, drivers and voluntary helpers. The way in which the nurse, attendant, hairdresser, or therapist addresses the person with aphasia can increase isolation and low self-esteem or consolidate inclusion and engagement. Fleeting moments and subtle aspects of communication and behaviour can make a profound difference.

Training is therefore needed not only to teach the mechanics of supporting communication but also to highlight and enable the expression of acknowledgement and respect. This would involve identifying how different attitudes and values are evident in day-to-day interactions with people who struggle to communicate, both at home and in different service settings. It would involve scrutinising the values and relationships that underpin policy and practice in service delivery, and identifying practical and achievable strategies for change. There was much evidence in the study of the exercise of institutional power, particularly in the context of hard-pressed, over-subscribed and poorly resourced services. Changing cultures, institutions and ways of speaking and behaving that have perhaps been taken for granted for decades is no easy task, however motivated the personnel. Training at the grass roots should not therefore be conducted in isolation from efforts to influence policy and planning.

Encouragingly, within the context of healthcare services attention is increasingly being paid to the processes of service delivery and to the underpinning social relations. Particular emphasis falls on the need for inclusive practices, underpinned by respectful and competent communication. The move towards partnership and shared decision-making in the delivery of health and other services will in time change the power balance of relationships within these domains. One of the outcomes of such a change might be the move towards providing services that are more geared to the concerns of service users, more relevant and therefore more effective. Charles' experience in the physiotherapy department suggests that, although listening to people with severe aphasia is not easy, understanding their perspective would enable service providers to be more effective and efficient. Those who cannot communicate cannot advocate for such changes, but there is a clear need for audit of communication practices at every level of provision, in every type of service.

Considering the personal response and the inner state of people affected by severe aphasia, the need for different levels of acknowledgement and support is clear. Counselling can be made accessible, enabling people with marked communication difficulties to articulate and address emotional issues (Clarke, in press). Exploring and sharing personal history and life stories with people who cannot communicate might also support the maintenance of a robust sense of personal identity, integration with family and community life and continuity with the past. This seems particularly important for people with aphasia in residential or nursing care, who may not have family members around them acting as guardians of their life stories. Inevitably, this kind of work on personal narrative would demand considerable skill and delicacy: another useful focus for training. Methods of supporting the identities of people with aphasia through narrative and portfolio work are currently being developed (Pound *et al*, 2000).

Accessible work, education and leisure opportunities would also strengthen and affirm identities, as would access to opportunities for contact with other people in similar situations. Members of the aphasia working group emphasised the importance of providing and fostering opportunities for people with severe language impairments to meet together, to share experiences, and to engage in purposeful activity. Aphasia self-help organisations and some voluntary sector organisations may be starting to address these issues, but the survey suggests that many have some way to go before people with severe language difficulties have access to their activities and can be fully included and engaged. Practical ideas for promoting communication access can be found in Pound and Hewitt (in press).

Relatives and friends of people with severe aphasia identified a need for training in the practical skills of supporting communication. Alongside this, they articulated a desire for acknowledgement of their own life changes and support in surmounting the barriers they face: for example, in accessing benefits. Some close relatives made the point that they themselves are excluded and isolated but are reluctant to privilege their own concerns at the expense of their loved one's needs. So although they do have a voice, it may seldom be heard.

Opportunity and access

In terms of infrastructure, the study indicates that employment opportunities for people with aphasia are minimal. Communication access to such opportunities (and to opportunities for training and education) could be enhanced, thereby making it possible for the person with aphasia to meet their potential and contribute their expertise and knowledge in paid or voluntary work (Parr *et al*, in press; Hewitt & Byng, in press). Clearly there is much work to be done with employers, trainers, educators, policy makers and providers of health and social care, voluntary and public services to raise awareness of aphasia and the disabling barriers faced by those who struggle to communicate. A useful focus for services currently expending energy and resources on activities that seem to miss the mark could be the identification, with people who have aphasia, of relevant work and educational and financial opportunities and working together to enhance their accessibility.

The study indicates that people with severe aphasia are faced with long periods of enforced 'leisure time', yet their access to leisure pursuits such as information and communication technology and reading may be very limited. Boredom seemed to be an issue for a number of participants. The importance of the television was very clear in this study, but this was often the only form of leisure activity people could access. Attention needs to be given to exploring and enhancing physical and communication access to a range of different leisure pursuits, such as sporting activities, literature and art, cooking and using computers. Services need to connect with the day-to-day lives of people with aphasia, the problems and restrictions they and their families face, and the issues of access that are raised across the spectrum of work, education and leisure (Pound & Hewitt, in press).

The study highlighted a disconnection between the various services used by people with aphasia. Thus, occupational therapists had no contact with disability employment services, even though their treatment focused on vocational activities. Speech and language therapists did not communicate with day centre staff or residential home personnel working on a day-to-day basis with people with severe aphasia. Voluntary sector groups providing services for people with aphasia had little to do with other community enterprises or with aphasia self-help groups. It is possible to live for many years with aphasia, and the person will pass through many different care settings during that time. More active and purposeful co-ordination

between providers of health, rehabilitation, welfare, community, voluntary and social services would enable good practice to be shared and aims and values to be articulated and have a beneficial impact on the long-term experience of people with aphasia.

The fact that discrimination against disabled people in employment and the delivery of services is now unlawful in the UK (Action for Dysphasic Adults, 1998) may prove a useful vehicle for change. By law, disabled people have equal access to employment, to services and to information about services. For people with aphasia, this means that communication access becomes a right, rather than a desirable add-on. When service users have aphasia, this means service providers need to learn how to support communication and to invest time in adapting information. This raises a number of resource issues: the process of supporting communication and enhancing access takes time and skill, and depends on training (Pound & Hewitt, in press).

Attention to the environment

Other infrastructural changes might facilitate the inclusion of people with severe aphasia. Institutional geography – the way in which space is laid out, organised, maintained and used – can enforce isolation and disempowerment, or it can increase respect, engagement and control. The alcove in which Albert passed many hours in his nursing home seemed to consolidate his remote status as someone who could not talk. Re-arranging seating and tackling background noise are simple processes that could make a big difference. Sitting down and talking with people who have aphasia is a simple but significant activity that could be prioritised in various health, institutional and voluntary care settings. While physical access to public and institutional space has improved, attention now needs to be paid to how environments can be designed and used in such a way as to maximise communication access.

People with aphasia who enter hospital, respite or residential care may not be able to ask someone to switch the lights or tv on or off, to change tv channels or to work the radio, and they may not be physically able to do this for themselves. Other forms of entertainment and passing time, such as reading, may be impossible. Frank, sitting in his respite room, wanted to listen to the radio, but it was broken. He wanted to watch tv but the old set had no remote control and he could not move from his chair to turn it on or off. He could not ask anyone to help him. His control of his environment and how he passed his time was profoundly compromised. Attention to these seemingly small details, being mindful of what someone like Frank might want, need, or enjoy, could make a big difference to the quality of his experience.

Attention to the environment also means ensuring that institutional spaces are cared for and well maintained. The unwatered, dying pot plants and the shabby fittings and fitments in Frank's room conveyed a careless attitude and added to the dismal atmosphere of the place. Brenda's room at her nursing home, in contrast, felt bright, orderly, clean and well cared for. The things she needed during the day were within her reach. She was surrounded by photos and mementos of home and family life. Her tv was new, and she had a remote control that worked. Attention to the 'nature of the place' also means thinking about the message, quality and tone

of notices, signs and other written material, with the purpose of ensuring they are physically and communicatively accessible and that they express respect. Small environmental changes of this kind could be effected with relative ease, yet could have a massive impact.

This project identified a number of influences that combine to constitute the experience of severe aphasia. The study suggests that severe aphasia is not so much a set of linguistic difficulties or inabilities as an experience that is largely shaped by how other people behave and interact within different systems, cultures and settings. At the final meeting of the advisory panel of people with aphasia, the comment was made that everyone with aphasia experiences, to a greater or lesser degree, problems of isolation, powerlessness, vulnerability and exclusion, not just those whose communication is severely compromised.

Language and communication may be severely restricted by aphasia. But the severity of the impact for the individual is determined by the response and behaviour of families, friends, statutory and voluntary service providers, communities and institutions. This study shows that, even though it is a regrettably common experience, social exclusion is not inevitable: people with severe aphasia can have access to choice, opportunity and engagement. This must influence policy, research, training and therapy. What happens to people with severe aphasia can be as enabling or disabling as the impairment itself.

References

Action for Dysphasic Adults (1998) *Open hole the stony wall: report of the ADA Working Party on the Disability Discrimination Act, 1995.* London: ADA.

Allen K (2000) *Communication and consultation: exploring ways for staff to involve people with dementia in developing services.* Bristol: The Policy Press and the Joseph Rowntree Foundation.

Barnes C, Mercer G (eds) (1997) *Doing disability research.* Leeds: The Disability Press.

Barnes C, Oliver M, Barton L (2002) *Disability studies today.* London: Polity Press.

Clarke H (2003) Doing less, being more. In: Parr S, Duchan J, Pound C (eds) *Aphasia inside out.* Maidenhead: Open University Press/McGraw Hill Education.

Code C (2000) *The incidence and prevalence of aphasia following stroke.* London: Speakability.

Davies C (1999) *Reflexive ethnography.* London: Routledge.

Department of Health (2001) *National service framework for older people.* London: Department of Health.

Edgar I, Russell A (1998) *The anthropology of welfare.* London: Routledge.

Hammersley M, Atkinson P (1995) *Ethnography: principles in practice.* 2nd edition. London: Routledge.

Hewitt A, Byng S (2003) Doors and windows: routes to engagement. In: Parr S, Duchan J, Pound C (eds) (2003) *Aphasia inside out: reflections on communication disability.* Maidenhead: Open University Press/McGraw Hill Education.

Kagan A (1998) Supported conversation for adults with aphasia. Clinical forum. *Aphasiology* **12** 816–830.

Layder D (1993) *New strategies in social research.* Oxford: Polity Press.

Oliver M. (1997) Emancipatory research: realistic goal or impossible dream? In: Barnes C, Mercer G (eds) (1997) *Doing disability research.* Leeds: The Disability Press.

Parr S, Byng S, Gilpin S *et al* (1997) *Talking about aphasia.* Buckingham: Open University Press.

Parr S, Duchan J, Pound C (eds) (2003) *Aphasia inside out: reflections on communication disability.* Maidenhead: Open University Press/McGraw Hill Education.

Parr S, Paterson K, Pound C (2003) Time please! temporal barriers in aphasia. In: Parr S, Duchan J, Pound C (eds) *Aphasia inside out: reflections on communication disability.* Maidenhead: Open University Press/McGraw Hill Education.

Pound C, Parr S, Lindsay J *et al* (2000) *Beyond aphasia: therapies for living with communication disability.* Bicester: Winslow Press.

Pound C, Hewitt A (in press) Communication barriers: building access and identity. In: Swain J, French S, Barnes C *et al* (eds) *Disabling barriers, enabling environments.* Maidenhead: Open University Press/McGraw Hill Education.

Ritchie J, Spencer L (1994) Qualitative data analysis for applied policy research. In: Bryman A, Burgess A (eds) *Analysing qualitative data.* London: Routledge.

Savage J (2000) Ethnography and health care. *British Medical Journal* **321** 1400–1402.

Spradley J (1980) *The ethnographic interview.* New York: Holt, Rheinhart and Winston.

Townsley R, Howarth J, Graham M *et al* (2002) *Committed to change? promoting the involvement of people with learning difficulties in staff recruitment.* Bristol: The Policy Press and Joseph Rowntree Foundation.

Zarb G (1997) Researching disabling barriers. In: Barnes C, Mercer G (eds) (1997) *Doing disability research.* Leeds: The Disability Press.

Websites

www.socialexclusionunit.gov.uk (accessed 10/9/03)

www.lic.gov.uk/publications/policyreports/inclusion (accessed 10/9/03)

Appendix One
Living with communication difficulties

Living with communication difficulties

Can you **help** us with a research project?

After a stroke, some people struggle to **talk and communicate**.

We'd like to find out about **your** experience of this:

- What are the **difficulties** you face?

- What would make life **easier**?

- How are you **managing**?

This may help us to make **services better**.

What will happen, if I agree?

Susie Parr, the researcher,
will come and visit you
in your own home and tell
you more about the project..

Then she will come and visit you
three times.

She'll sit quietly with you
and observe what happens...

3 visits...

sitting quietly...

while you get on.

If you **go out**, she might come with you....

She'll talk to you
and ask you about **your experience.**

She'll also talk to a person who has
contact with you....

That person will be asked to keep a **diary**
of everyday events for a short period...

If you agree, you may want to **video** some everyday events...

What will happen to the research?

At the end of the project, the results will be written up in a **report**.

You will be **given a copy** of the report.

The results may be:

- **published**

- used in **teaching** or at **conferences**.

Your name will **NOT** be used at any time.

What are the benefits?

The research will help people to know more about the **difficulties** you face

It may help us to **improve services**

It may **help other people** in the same situation as you.

What are the disadvantages?

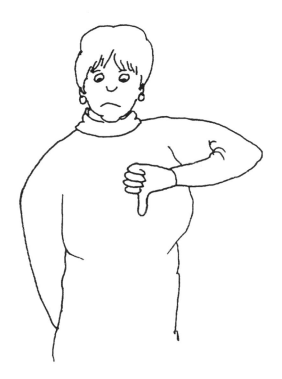

Sometimes you may not want Susie to visit you. She will always **check** with you first.

This is **not** therapy... it **won't** make your talking better.

If you agree to take part:

It's **ok to stop**.
You can pull out at any time.
It's your choice.

Thank you
Susie Parr
(0117) 921 1192

Consent Form

- I have seen the **information booklet** about this research project.

 yes 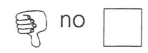 no

- I have **talked** with Susie Parr about the project. We have looked at the information together and **my questions have been answered**.

 yes no

- I know about the **project** and I **understand** what is involved.

 yes no

- I understand that, if I decide to take part, it is **my free choice**.

 yes  no

- I understand that I am free to **pull out** at any time and any treatment I have will **not** be affected.

 yes   no

- **I agree** to take part in the above study.

 yes   no

Name of person agreeing to take part

Date   Signature

Name of person taking/witnessing consent

Date   Signature

Audio/Visual Release Form

- I agree to be recorded on **audio** tape.

☐ 👍 yes  👎 no ☐

- I agree to be recorded on **video** tape.

☐ 👍 yes 👎 no ☐

- I agree that the tapes may be used for **teaching** and **research**. I will not be named or identified.

☐ 👍 yes 👎 no ☐

Witnessed by

Signed   **Signed**

┌──────────────────────┐   ┌──────────────────────┐
│   │   │   │
└──────────────────────┘   └──────────────────────┘

Date   *Date*

┌──────────────────────┐   ┌──────────────────────┐
│   │   │   │
└──────────────────────┘   └──────────────────────┘

Appendix Two
Excerpts from ethnographic field notes

Terry in respite care

I reach Terry's room: a single room with a single hospital bed in it (it is high, has wheels and ratchets and side bars which are dropped down). His name is written in biro on a piece of paper sellotaped to the wall just above the bed. There is an anglepoise lamp over the bed, a locker, an old brown Parker Knoll armchair with a pair of underpants and a baseball hat on it, a small tv. The window looks onto a patch of grass and a wall. A wire coat hanger hangs from a hook on the wall. The room feels odd. It is shabby, bare, flaking light pink paintwork, yet with a gaily coloured geometric frieze around the top and similarly gaily patterned duvet on the unmade bed. An open door leads into another room: a long tiled room with a washbasin and a disabled toilet at the end, with grab rails and bars around it. It feels dingy.

Interpretation: The wallpaper and duvet can't hide the hospital feel. It is a place for people who are sick or with motor impairments, unlike Terry. The dinginess and shabbiness adds another aspect. It makes the room feel like a hostel for homeless people.

Personal: I would so hate having to stay here, were I in Terry's position.

I think Terry has been having a rest, his bed is rumpled, the duvet thrown back. 'Come on then,' says Terry, smiling. He is rather shaky, his hands trembling, and I wonder if this is because he has just woken up. Or does he need to take some medication? He pats his duvet, but I move the underpants and hat and sit on the armchair facing the bed. He sits on the bed. 'How are you getting on here Terry?' I ask. He's been here nearly two weeks. 'It's alright, it's alright' he says with an uncertain intonation ... 'but'... long drawn out... 'but'... He trails off. I look round the room. 'When are you going home?' He struggles: 'Um...um... come on, come on...' 'Tomorrow?' I ask. 'No.' He picks up a tv times and searches through the pages until he comes to Monday and shows me. 'Looking forward to going home?' 'Oh yes,' he says.

Terry at home

I can see on the planner (and remember from my phone conversation with his wife) that he has just been in Meerwood House again for respite. I check this with him. He nods and I ask how it was. He grimaces. 'It's alright, it's alright,' he says doubtfully. 'But...' and this word trails off uncertainly and he shrugs. Was his friend Steve there? 'Yes, yes.' He writes: '13 Nov.' I look at November 13 on the planner and the same tiny writing reads: 'Terry respite.' He says: 'Him and me,' pointing to the chair where Jane his wife sat last time I visited. 'Alright, alright. But...' then he mimes a conflict, grabbing at his own throat and grimacing and saying 'Oooh.' Then he says in a conciliatory tone: 'It's alright though. Him and me. But...' and he clenches his two fists and bangs them together. I say: 'You get on ok, you and Jane but you need a rest, from each other?' and he says: 'That's it. That's it.'

I remember the stark, dingy bedroom at Meerwood House and say: 'Do you prefer to be at home?' He grimaces again: 'Well', again with an uncertain intonation. He jumps up again, goes out and comes back with a spiral bound notebook and a biro. He writes: 'JOPS.' and says: 'Better, this. It's all gone you see. All gone.' 'You want to work?' I venture. 'That's it. That's it. But it's all gone.' He points round the room to all the furniture, which his wife had told me he made before his stroke. 'It's gone.' He mimes sleeping, by resting his cheek on the back of his hand. 'Over there, that's it. That's it.' I ask what he will do today and he shrugs and then makes a pulling movement with his hand and points to the window. 'Over there.' I think for a minute. 'Fishing?' No. He makes a repetitive, side-to-side movement with his hand and points out of the window: 'That'. The hedge is waving wildly and I say: 'Trim the hedge?' and he says: 'That's it that's it.' With an electric trimmer?' I ask. 'Yes.' What will he have for lunch? He mimes a chicken by tucking his hands into his armpits, raising and lowering his elbows and clucking. 'Chicken?' 'That's it.' What sort of chicken? He shrugs, he doesn't know. He says: 'Fried chicken?' He points to Jane's chair and says: 'Him.' 'Something Jane has left for you?' 'Yes.' Then what? tv? He smiles and says: 'Yes' and leaning forward grabs a TV Times and shows me the write-up of a film about Grace Kelly, on Channel 5 at 3pm. 'Good. Good?' He mimes sleep again and I say: 'Will you go to sleep?' and he says 'Yes.' He points to his head with a finger and makes a circular movement, then mimes eating something from his hand, then sleep. 'You take tablets that make you sleepy?' 'That's it,' and in he goes to the kitchen again, coming back with a Flora margarine container full of tablets that he shows me. Epilin, Lamital, Fluoxetine, Baclofen (when he shows me this he rubs all down his right side) and aspirin (he pats his heart). 'When do you go to sleep?' He points to his watch, to the 3 and then the 4. 'Him and him. More or less.' 'Is it ok being here on your own? It seems like a long day.' He frowns and says: 'It's alright, but...' and then he points to 'JOPS' in his notebook. 'It's all gone.'

Appendix Three
Sample analytic chart

Features and impact of the environment	TERRY	BRENDA	FRANK	ROGER
Physical environment	Respite environment dominated by needs of those with motor and mobility impairments: not at all suitable for T, who only has aphasia. (b1-2)	Wheelchair, problem with footplate painfully pressed against her calf that she can't draw attention to. (a4)	Frank's physical needs means that his living space is full of equipment (a1) (c4) and even at home the room feels hospital like. He often seems uncomfortable, shifting in his chair…(b7) Mrs Stock describes the problems with helping Frank out of the house: heavy chair, tight turn on ramp, her back gives way.	Roger has few physical impairments, and does not attend day centres etc. He goes out and does shopping, goes bowling. Brenda sets him up to work on the computer at home.
Type and feel of environment	'Loaded up' on social services day centre bus with people he does not know. (a9) Respite room dingy (b1) and shabby, feels like a hostel for homeless people. Poor quality furniture. Home is constant reminder of what he can no longer do: all his tools and things he has made. (c8)	Room at the home spotless, orderly, filled with mementoes and pictures. Cosy, personal feel. (b5) Hot and smelly dining room, flies, urine. (a4) Noises off… people crying 'nurse help me nurse help me' over and over. (b7)	Ward room in respite is clinical, noisy, smells waft in, dingy, unwatered pot plants. (b2) Hospital equipment everywhere in respite centre: charts, oxygen cylinders, hoists etc. (b3) Can't get out without knowing the combination numbers. (b7)	Orderly, homely and cosy in his home. Fantastic window boxes filled with flowers. (a2)

Note: Letters and numbers refer to sets of observation notes (a, b or c) and page numbers

Features and impact of the environment	TERRY	BRENDA	FRANK	ROGER
Dissonance	Respite care leaflet talks about 'first class, 24 hour care' but Terry often alone. Shabby environment. (b4)	'Fresh produce carefully prepared by our chef' belies powdered chicken soup served in plastic bowls the same colour to some residents. Others get china bowls. Evaporated milk separating in the heat. Whole place feels quite plush but then budget lemonade served in plastic glasses and food poor. No choice, no salt and pepper, no vinegar for chips and Brenda can't ask. (b4) Little evidence of choice.		
Communication environment	Computer room very noisy. (a6)	Phone rings unanswered. (a6) Noise of tv very loud. (b4) Nurses call and chat to each other but apart don't interact with residents other than to offer food and assistance. (a6) Acker Bilk CD played very loud at lunchtime. (a6)	Frank is seated beside wall in respite room, far from window and can't reach tv. (b1) Using writing as a means of communication is physically awkward, balancing the book on high, wobbly hospital table. Effortful and exhausting. (b4)	Varies wherever he goes. Ritualised encounters of the bowls club seem to be helpful and he becomes invisible, one of the gang. (b2) Team mates communicate directly, tease him, tell jokes and Roger fits in. Wendy describes how she has had to encourage the kids to involve him in their conversations about the day....

Note: Letters and numbers refer to sets of observation notes (a, b or c) and page numbers

Features and impact of the environment	TERRY	BRENDA	FRANK	ROGER
Spoken environment	IT tutor talks very fast (a3) using loads of jargon. Steve's instructions difficult to follow: Terry gets angry trying to print out some clip art. (b8)	One nurse extremely polite and attentive, asking people if they would like help, and saying 'you're welcome' when thanked. (a4)	I rarely see anyone address Frank directly, only his wife and daughter to do with physical care. People bringing the WRVS trolley ask his daughter if he would like anything, not him. (a4)	Jokes and innuendoes may be inaccessible, as is some conversation but all swept along by bonhomie and ritual. (b6)
Written environment	Leaflets in day centre incomprehensible. (a1-2) Notices in computer room jargon filled. (c4) Respite care blurb wordy. (b4) Notices on respite wall rather authoritarian: 'Have you cleaned up?' (b5)	Mission statement on wall of reception, together with photo of extremely elderly resident in bed, nurses grouped around (a1) plus some religious icons. Whiteboard has today's menu. (a3) Many decorative texts on walls of Brenda's room. (b4)	Frank's name written in biro on a scrap of paper and sellotaped to bed head in respite. Very 'hospital' feel eg. 'dirty utility' written on door opposite Frank's room. (b5)	
Technology type	Portable communication aid. (a3) Computer at day centre and in respite care. (b8) Home computer. (c3)	Tv and video. Remote control. (b5)	Uses tv and radio at home. Uses remote to flick through channels. But ancient black and white tv in respite has no remote. Radio doesn't work. He sits for hours doing 'nothing much'. (b6) Communication file. (b4)	Communication aid. (a2) Home PC. (c7) Camera. (c6)

Note: Letters and numbers refer to sets of observation notes (a, b or c) and page numbers

Features and impact of the environment	TERRY	BRENDA	FRANK	ROGER
Why and why not used	Highly dependent on help and support as randomly hits buttons trying to make computers work. (b8 and c3) Can't follow written instructions. Spoken instructions need to be step-by-step, slow, clear. Often they're not.		Radio broken. Can't reach tv. (b6)	All used but needs pretty constant support from Wendy. (c7)
Communication aids	Communication aid, uses this to signal area of conversation.	None evident.	Not used because no one seems to know about it, or encourage it. Also physically difficult and unwieldy. (b5) No paper and pen available. (a4)	Computer...portable aid. (a2) Useful to indicate area of message but then lots of guessing and background knowledge necessary. Wendy has learned how to programme it. (a11)
Other	Exhausting process of trying to print out clipart creation... rapid, seemingly random button hitting and a lot of frustration. (c3)	Director of home and tea man walk into Brenda's room without knocking. (a10)		
Exclusion/ inclusion?	Isolated in his room at respite care. (b1) Home environment full of reminders of his working life: tools and artefacts. (c8)	No real engagement between residents and nurses. (a7) Brenda seems sequestered away in her room.	Frank has quite a lot of control and engagement at home but seems very isolated and bored at the respite centre. The environment tells him he is definitely a 'patient' and there is also a security/ prison-like feel as no one can get out without punching in the correct numbers.	Sense of Roger being included. He forays out into the neighbourhood, to post office and fish and chip shop and bowls club. Sense that Wendy is offering constant yet unobtrusive support to enable this to happen.

Note: Letters and numbers refer to sets of observation notes (a, b or c) and page numbers